Overcoming
Compulsive
Desires

Overcoming Compulsive Desires

Lester + Sumrall

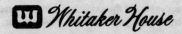
Whitaker House

OVERCOMING COMPULSIVE DESIRES

ISBN: 0-88368-337-7
Printed in the United States of America
Copyright© 1990 by Lester Sumrall Evangelistic
Association, Inc.

Whitaker House
580 Pittsburgh Street
Springdale, PA 15144

CONTENTS

Part I: The Struggle

Part II: The Victory

PART I:
THE STRUGGLE

ONE

CAUGHT
IN THE GRIP
OF DESIRE

In February 1988 noted TV evangelist Jimmy Swaggart confessed to engaging in sexual sin with a prostitute, and later evidence suggested this was a habitual practice. When his denomination's leaders, as part of their disciplinary action, told him to stay out of the pulpit longer than he wanted, he defied them and went back early. What causes a man of God, one who has led thousands to Christ, to risk his reputation and ministry that way?

The year before, the ministry of Jim Bakker, head of the PTL network, was brought down by the revelation of his sexual sin and financial misdeeds. In earlier times, even when he was regularly going on the air to plead for money to save the ministry from bankruptcy, he and his wife were spending thousands upon thousands of dollars on clothes, cars and jewelry. In late 1989 he was convicted of multiple financial crimes in his raising and spending of ministry funds. Why does a Jim Bakker do such things?

Also in 1987, Gordon MacDonald, the popular president of Inter-Varsity Christian Fellowship, resigned from his position when the news got out that he had indulged in an extramarital affair. What made him hurt his wife that way and put a scar on the church of Jesus Christ?

The year 1988 also saw the early end of the presidential candidacy of Gary Hart after his adultery became public knowledge. At the time he was considered the leader in the race for the Democratic Party's nomination. Why would he ruin his chances for our country's highest office in exchange for a few hours of sinful pleasure?

In late 1986 investor Ivan Boesky admitted he was guilty of buying and selling stock based on illegally obtained information. As part of his punishment, he agreed to pay the government a fine of $100 million and never to trade on the stock market again. Why would a man who had already enjoyed great success and amassed a fortune others only dream of continue to engage in criminal activity just to make his wealth grow larger and larger?

Famous people like these get all the headlines, of course, but they're hardly unique in letting sinful desires get the best of them. For example, a Canadian lady writing in the January 1988 issue of *Decision* magazine tells the story of how she grew more and more attracted to Doug, a man in her office. She was happily married, and, as she writes, "infidelity was the furthest thing from my mind."

Nonetheless, she enjoyed Doug's ego-boosting compliments, and "soon I was telling him my personal problems and revealing confidences that should have been shared with my husband alone. Before I knew it, a fantasy had developed in my mind. At first it happened occasionally, but it reached a point where my thought life centered on this man. I began mentally to rehearse details of an affair with Doug. Fidelity toward my husband looked colorless in comparison to the inviting relationship I could be having. To add to the temptation, Doug was suggesting meetings outside working hours."

Fortunately (or maybe we should say providentially), this lady stopped the relationship before ending up in bed with Doug, and in later chapters we'll look at how she broke the grip of the compulsive desire that was threatening to ruin her life. But my point here is that we're *all* vulnerable to the lures of compulsive desires, including ordinary Christians like this woman.

The sad facts are that Americans spend $8 billion on pornography each year, and one hundred new pornographic videos are released each week. An estimated six billion hours of working time are lost each year in the United States due to alcoholism. Our people squandered about $22 billion in state lotteries in 1985, and to that you can add the billions of dollars in legal casino gambling and all the forms of illegal betting.

Sorry to say, those statistics are only the tip of the iceberg. We could cite many more showing our common addictions to cocaine and other illegal (and legal) drugs, to shopping for unneeded things and using ever larger amounts of debt to get what we want right away, to out-of-control eating that leads to obesity and endangers our health, and so on. I think it's safe to say we live in a society whose people are dominated by compulsive desires.

An Ancient Problem

But let's not make the mistake of thinking the surrender to sinful desires is something new. Scripture gives us many clear examples of the same thing. For example, mighty Samson gave up his strength and ultimately his life because he was obsessed with a heathen woman. Even though Delilah was shockingly obvious in her wish to see Samson captured by the enemy Philistines, he was blinded by his lust and arrogance and handed himself over like a lamb led to slaughter.

The rich young ruler turned his back on salvation because he loved his money more than the Christ who told him to give it all away and become His disciple. He had a noble urge to follow the Lord, but the control of materialism was stronger. Jesus described this type of compulsive desire perfectly in the parable of the sower: "Now he who received seed among the thorns is he who hears the word [of God], and the cares of this world and the deceitfulness of riches choke the word, and he becomes unfruitful" (Matt. 13:22).

Foolish Nabal threw away his own life and risked the lives of his family and servants, because in his drunkenness and greed he refused to help David, God's anointed king. David and his men had protected rich Nabal's flocks and workers. Yet he rudely refused to share his food with David and insulted him at the same time. And while David was preparing to avenge his honor, Nabal was feasting like a king and getting drunk as a skunk. Only the wise intercession of Nabal's wife, Abigail, saved his entire household from destruction.

The ultimate in compulsive sinful desire ruling people's lives is pictured in Romans 1. There the apostle Paul described people who, "although they knew God, they did not glorify Him as God, nor were thankful, but became futile in their thoughts, and their foolish hearts were darkened....Therefore God also gave them up to uncleanness, in the lusts of their hearts, to dishonor their bodies among themselves,... being filled with all unrighteousness, sexual immorality, wickedness, covetousness, maliciousness, full of envy, murder, strife, deceit, evil-mindedness..." (Rom. 1:21,24,29). The list goes on and on, showing clearly how vile people can be when their lives are dominated by compulsive desires.

In most cases, when people give in to their wrongful

urges, they know they're doing wrong. As Romans 1 points out, "Although they knew God...." Yet they go ahead and sin anyway. Why? The simple answer is that the desire to sin is stronger than the desire to obey and please God. And once a person gives in to temptation and chooses to break God's law, it becomes even easier to do it the next time and the next. Before long, the sin becomes a habit, and then the habit begins to control the person. The end result is a compulsive, overwhelming desire and a life of spiritual defeat.

The Bible describes the process this way in James 1:14-15: "But each one is tempted when he is drawn away by his own desires and enticed. Then, when desire has conceived, it gives birth to sin"—habitual, ongoing sin—"and sin, when it is full-grown"—when it's grown into a compulsion—"brings forth death."

A wise man once said much the same thing in these words: "We first make our habits, and then our habits make us." Pastor and writer A.W. Tozer put it this way: "We are all the sum total of our hungers." And those whose habits and hungers are dominated by sinful compulsions are on a sure path to spiritual ruin.

Now the Good News

Now that we've identified the problem, it's time for me to give you the good news. Although the temptation to sin and to get wrapped up in compulsive desires is always around us, we don't have to be defeated. Victory is possible! The God who loves us and wants only the best for His children has made a way for us to live free from compulsive, controlling desires and be subject only to Him. And in this book I want to share that plan of victory and freedom with you.

Our approach to presenting that plan is simple. In the first part of the book we'll look at why we're so vulnerable to compulsive desires, how they control us, why God doesn't just deliver us from them immediately, and what role our emotions play. In the second part we'll consider the steps God has provided on the path to freedom. We'll see that the way isn't easy, but that with the Spirit's help we *can* reach the goal.

Not only can we reach the goal, but it's God's will for us, and what He wants for us He'll guide us and empower us to do. As we read in 1 Corinthians 10:13, "No temptation has overtaken you except such as is common to man; but God is faithful, who will not allow you to be tempted beyond what you are able, but with the temptation will also make the way of escape, that you may be able to bear it."

So join me as we learn about compulsive desire and how we can enjoy the Lord's victory over it. We'll begin in the next chapter by seeing just what it is and what kinds of sinful desire tend to dominate people's lives today.

TWO

DESIRES WE CAN'T CONTROL

What are some of the compulsive desires that commonly enslave people today? Consider the following examples, and see if you recognize in any of them your struggles or those of folks you know.

Moira, a slender seventeen-year-old in white cowboy boots, goes to meetings of a group called Overeaters Anonymous three times a week. Why? She's never been fat, yet she used to throw up four times a day. "I can eat anything with these hands," she says.

Here's how Moira explains her craving for food: "Start with Sara Lee lemon pie, move on to a gallon of ice cream and brownie mix straight from the box.

At school I sit in class counting my money, listing what I'm going to buy. And then I figure out what I can steal from the 7-Eleven on the way home.'"

Encouraged by the more than $2 billion the food industry spends on advertising each year, millions of Americans eat to excess and are overweight. Ninety percent of the diets we try are doomed to fail, and a large majority of even our young people can't pass a basic fitness test because they're overweight and out of shape. The diet aid, diet food, diet TV show and diet book businesses continue to thrive year after year because we know we weigh too much, yet we can't push ourselves away from the dining room table.

A Losing Bet

Another out-of-control desire dominating many people today is compulsive gambling, and the opportunities to wager are multiplying rapidly. New casinos are going up every day in Nevada and Atlantic City, and at the time of this writing, voters in Gary, Indiana, recently approved casino gambling there. Then we have horse and dog tracks, off-track betting, illegal bookmakers handling everything from political elections to boxing matches to college football games, and the growing number of state lotteries.

People caught in the grip of compulsive gambling have a tremendous ability to deceive themselves, to go on believing that the next bet will result in a big win and boost them into a life of luxury and ease—despite losses piled upon losses. A compulsive gambler remembers parking at New York's Aqueduct racetrack one day and reacting this way: "I looked at the stands, and there were sixty thousand people in there. I had six dollars in my pocket and I owed ten thousand dollars. And I was thinking, Look at all those people there—and I'll be taking home all their money."[2]

When a gambler's spouse loses patience and forces him to face his addiction (compulsive gambling is largely a male problem), and he pleads with her not to leave and promises he'll change, "he is not thinking how hard he is going to try this time to give it up....He is thinking about what else he can say to manipulate her. He is agonizing about not being able to get back to his gambling," says an authority in the field.[3]

Clearly, this is a habit that takes control of people and deprives them of the ability to think logically and make good decisions. As a wise person once observed, "The chains of habit are too weak to be felt until they are too strong to be broken."

Can This Be Love?

Most of us are familiar with Shakespeare's famous story about Romeo and Juliet. It glamorizes romantic love and supposedly shows the depth of devotion such love can inspire. But what it really shows is the depth of foolishness that compulsive desire for another person can inspire.

To refresh your memory, Romeo and Juliet were

teenage lovers from feuding families, and their parents and kin were so opposed to the match that Juliet felt she had to resort to trickery for them to be together. While Romeo was away in hiding, and with the help of a potion from a kindhearted but misguided priest, Juliet pretended to die. The plan was that Romeo would come back secretly, revive her and take her away for a happily-ever-after life in some far-off place.

Unfortunately, Romeo got the news of Juliet's "death" before he got the message that it was only a ploy, and he raced to her tomb convinced she was really gone. When he saw her lying on her bier, he was so overcome with grief that, after a flowery speech about how life wasn't worth living without his beautiful Juliet, he drank some poison and died on the spot.

Shortly afterward, Juliet came out of her drug-induced deep sleep, saw Romeo dead on the floor next to her, made her own flowery speech about how life had no purpose without her handsome Romeo, and drank the rest of his poison. So ended tragically and senselessly two young lives full of promise.

Don't get me wrong: I believe in deep love between a man and a woman. It's one of God's great gifts to us, and my wife and I dearly love each other. But when a person becomes so infatuated with another that he can think of nothing else—when his hopes and plans and emotions are so wrapped up in his lover that life seems to have no value or reason for continuing apart from her—he's caught in a compulsive desire that's unhealthy any way you look at it. And the worst of the problem is that he's giving her a level of devotion and love that belongs by right only to God.

Sadly, this kind of romantic passion is what usually passes for love in our day. Two people see each other, are attracted physically, find they enjoy one another's company and quickly "fall in love." They don't stop to consider their different backgrounds, different values and different expectations of the relationship, and what it means to make and keep a lifetime commitment to your mate. It's no wonder our divorce rate is so high.

Money, Money

In the first chapter I wrote of Ivan Boesky as an example of someone with a compulsive desire for money. This is one of the most powerful desires, and it's running rampant in our materialistic, yuppie society. But there's truly nothing new under the sun, and we find a clear example of this back in the Old Testament book of Joshua.

In Joshua 6 we see how God gave the children of Israel a great victory at Jericho. He had instructed them in how to march around the city for seven days and then have the priests blow their trumpets on the seventh day. After that, the city's defensive walls fell down, and Israel stormed in and captured the city.

Part of God's instruction concerning the conquest was that the people of Israel were to take nothing of value from Jericho—no spoils of war. And this is where the trouble came in. One Hebrew man, Achan, disobeyed. He saw some gold, silver and beautiful clothes, and greed overcame him. He took the loot and hid it under his tent.

As a result, when Israel went into battle against the small city of Ai, God's people were dealt a shocking defeat. The Lord let them lose to a greatly inferior army because one man had disregarded His law. When He then led Joshua to Achan as the sinner, and Joshua asked for an explanation, Achan said, "When I saw among the spoils a beautiful Babylonian garment, two hundred shekels of silver, and a wedge of gold weighing fifty shekels, I coveted them and took them" (Josh. 7:21).

Here was a man willing to endanger not only himself, but also his family (they were all stoned to death as punishment) and the whole nation, in order to satisfy his desire for material possessions. Surely, as the Savior said, "Where your treasure is, there your heart will be also....No one can serve two masters....You cannot serve God and mammon" (Matt. 6:21,24). A person who loves money will do anything to get it, regardless of the consequences.

Nor is there such a thing as "enough" to the person in love with money. I mentioned earlier that Ivan Boesky was already very rich, yet he went on breaking the law to gain still more. The Hunt brothers down in Texas already had the billions left to them by their father when they almost lost everything trying to corner the world's silver market and become even richer.

Jesus captured this mindset perfectly in the parable of the rich fool. "The ground of a certain rich man yielded plentifully," He said. "And he thought within himself saying, 'What shall I do, since I have no more room to store my crops?' "

This man had so much he couldn't store it all—far more than enough to meet his needs. So what would he do? Give the excess away to feed the hungry? Sell it and present the proceeds to God as an offering of thanks? Endow a chair in economics at Jerusalem University? No, none of the above. "He said, 'I will do this: I will pull down my barns and build greater, and there I will store all my crops and my goods. And I will say to my soul, "Soul, you have many goods laid up for many years; take your ease; eat, drink, and be merry." ' " He would just hoard it all for himself and get fat and lazy—never mind God or the needs of others.

God's opinion of this man was brief and to-the-point: "You fool! This night your soul will be required of you; then whose will those things be which you have provided?" Jesus concluded by saying, "So is he who lays up treasure for himself, and is not rich toward God" (Luke 12:16-21).

Please understand that you don't have to be rich to be a slave to money and the things it can buy. The easy availability of credit cards has opened the door for millions of Americans to walk into deep debt, often finding themselves in serious trouble before they realize what's happened. The average American adult holds six credit cards. And with a few clothes here, a few presents there, an occasional meal out, and so on, the debts pile up quickly—often faster than they can be paid off. Surveys show that one out of every six people who use credit is in trouble with debt.

The basic problem for average people like these is the same as the one facing rich folks like Ivan Boesky; they're never satisfied with what they have. They always want more. They're not content to live within the means God provides, so they use credit to live beyond their incomes. And every year they fall further and further into the slavery of materialism fueled by debt.

There's a popular bumper sticker these days that summarizes the attitude of society: "He who dies with the most toys wins." But nothing could be further from the truth.

Look at Me

Still another common compulsive desire today is for self-exaltation. In a word, this is the sin of pride. It was, in fact, the original sin—it's what got Satan, one of God's angels, thrown out of heaven even before the creation of the human race. The Lord said of Lucifer (Satan), "For you have said in your heart: 'I will ascend into heaven, I will exalt my throne above the stars of God....I will ascend above the heights of the clouds, I will be like the Most High' " (Is. 14:13-14).

All of us are proud to one extent or another. If you ask a group of people to compare themselves to others, the great majority will say they're *above* average. (That must mean the few who are below average are really bad!). Now I don't mean to condemn the healthy sense of feeling good about ourselves that comes with a job well done or the realization of how much we mean to God. We're of great worth in His eyes or He wouldn't have put His Son through the experience of the cross to redeem us and make us His children.

The problem comes when we think more highly of ourselves than we ought, when we lose touch with the reality of our shortcomings and weaknesses—and especially when we start to think we're better than others.

There's a lady named Cassie who goes to church every Sunday, leads a very moral life and considers herself to be humble. Most people would agree with her self-assessment, yet she's friendless and lonely. Why? Because she considers herself to be just about perfect, and she worries that neighbors, co-workers and even fellow churchgoers will turn on her and hurt her when they recognize she's superior to them. So she doesn't let anyone close but instead feels persecuted by all the "jealous" people around her.[4]

There are many people like this in our churches. Their pride may be subtle, but it's very real and very strong, and they far outnumber the people whose pride is obvious for everyone to see.

We're All Vulnerable

I could spell out many other types of compulsive desires, including some that involve physical as well as emotional and psychological addiction—desires for pornography, for drugs or alcohol, for unnatural sex, for worshipping and pleasing Satan rather than God, and so on. But if you've examined your life honestly in light of the descriptions above, I think you'll agree that not one of us is immune to the appeal of compulsive desire. What tempts one person will be a little different from what tempts another, but in one or more areas we're *all* vulnerable.

Consider the great apostle Paul. Here was a mighty man of faith, a spiritual warrior, a teacher and evangelist without peer—the writer, under the Spirit's guidance, of about half our New Testament. He could say in complete honesty: "If anyone else thinks he may have confidence in the flesh, I more so" (Phil. 3:4). He was so confident of his faithfulness in living for the Lord that he could say, "Imitate me, just as I also imitate Christ" (1 Cor. 11:1). What a challenge! Near the end of his life he could also write, "I have fought the good fight, I have finished the race, I have kept the faith" (2 Tim. 4:7).

In spite of claiming all that, Paul was genuinely a humble man. As kids used to say, Paul was giving us no brag, just the facts. And yet we can't overlook the other side of the coin. In spiritual wisdom, maturity and obedience to the Lord, Paul was miles ahead of probably 99.9 percent of all the Christians who have ever lived. But he had to admit, "The good that I will to do, I do not do; but the evil I will not to do, that I practice....I find then a law, that evil is present with me, the one who wills to do good. For I delight in the law of God according to the inward man. But I see another law in my members, warring against the law of my mind, and *bringing me into captivity to the law of sin which is in my members*" (Rom. 7:19,21-23, my emphasis).

Even Paul battled with a compulsive desire of some kind. It brought him into captivity to sin. It caused him not to do good but to do evil instead. There was at least one temptation to which he was especially vulnerable. Was it bitterness? Anger? Covetousness? We don't know. The important thing for us to understand here is that if the apostle Paul was forced to struggle against a compulsive desire of whatever kind, how much more are we likely to have to struggle?

No doubt this is why Paul, in 1 Corinthians 10, listed several Old Testament examples of people who fell into sin, and then he wrote, "Therefore let him who thinks he stands take heed lest he fall" (v. 12). Never get so sure of your walk with God that you think you've got it made and could never stumble. It's happened to better men and women than you and I are; it could happen to anyone.

But I want to end this chapter on a positive note. There's hope for victory! Because all believers in all ages struggle with sinful desires, we can learn from their experiences. In the Bible and other testimonies we can see what works—the provision God has made for His children to enjoy spiritual triumph and not defeat. And as we continue to learn those lessons, we need to look next at just why it is that compulsive desires are able to enslave us.

THREE

WHY WE BECOME ENSLAVED

A certain preacher, writing in *Leadership* magazine, told of how he struggled for years with lust and an addiction to pornography. When he would travel to speak at some Christian gathering or other, which was often, he would take advantage of his out-of-town anonymity to buy pornographic magazines and visit adult movie theaters. On at least one occasion, in a large city, he visited a live sex show.

Did he know this activity was wrong? Yes. Did he understand his ministry and reputation, not to mention his marriage, could be destroyed if he were found out? Of course. Then why did he do it? What need in his life was being met by this form of illicit sexual gratification, a need so powerful that it led him to risk everything?

After reflecting on those questions, this is what the man wrote: "[Pornography] enticed me with the promise of relationship: Cheryl Tiegs and Madonna and the monthly Playmates would remove their clothes and smile at me from the pages of magazines....In sex, I want to feel welcome. I want to feel accepted, not rejected....

"I think most women would be surprised to learn how intimidating, even terrifying, sex is for many men. Pornography lowers the terror. It's an easy form of arousal. And the key to the arousal is the illusion of welcomeness....Beautiful women from around the globe smile at me, beckon me to enjoy them."[1]

All of us yearn for a close personal relationship with another—for intimacy. We long to know and love someone deeply. We really want to be committed to one person for life. Part of this desire is the sexual attraction between man and woman. This is a legitimate need God built into us as human beings, and as such it's a *good* thing.

At the same time, because this need is so powerful, it makes us extremely vulnerable. As that pastor pointed out, we can fear rejection almost as much as we want the fulfillment. And when the need gets wrapped up with the fear, especially in a person who's not good at developing close relationships (even though he may be married, as the pastor was), you have a prime candidate for addiction to lust and pornography.

Perverting the Good

As the story above demonstrates, compulsive sinful desires don't really have a life of their own. They don't spring out of thin air to lead us astray. Instead, they appeal to our natural, inborn, God-given needs. The needs themselves are legitimate, but sin uses them against us by offering illegitimate, substitute ways of getting them met—ways God never intended us to use. Sin takes what is good and perverts it.

In this chapter we want to look at what some of our genuine needs are and how they get distorted and turned against us. This understanding is vital to breaking sinful habits and finding the fulfillment of our needs in the good ways God has provided.

We've already seen how the need to be accepted by the opposite sex in a loving, committed relationship can be twisted. Another need is to be accepted by friends, co-workers and others who are close to us. This also can be turned into a sinful compulsive desire.

With young people we talk about peer pressure as a potential danger. Adolescents are so concerned about being "in" with their peers, especially if they don't feel accepted and affirmed at home, that they'll often do almost anything to win that acceptance. And whichever group offers it will also provide young people's unwritten code of attitude, dress and behavior. Research shows, in fact, that in recent years peers have replaced parents as the strongest influence in teens' lives.[2]

This is why it's so important to know whom our kids spend time with and to help them choose friends wisely. As youth ministry experts have learned, "Simply put, our children will become like the friends with whom they spend the most time."[3] If those friends use alcohol or other drugs, the chances are our kids will, too, despite all our efforts to the contrary. If those friends regularly view pornography or engage in premarital sex, shoplift, use profanity, smoke or chew tobacco, or indulge in any other disgusting or immoral habits, our children will likely do the same—all for the sake of being accepted by the gang.

"Wickedness loves company—and leads others into sin" (Prov. 16:29, TLB). People who aren't ashamed of their wickedness, or who have been convinced by our godless society that what they're doing isn't even wrong, will always try to get those around them to participate with them. It's a fact of human nature we can't get around. And when these people are the leaders of social groups, the kind of peer pressure that will exist there is all too predictable.

What's true of young people is also true of adults. We can be just as prone to following the crowd as our adolescents. So we also need to be careful about whom we choose as our close friends. This is why alcoholics and drug addicts usually need to break off old friendships and find new ones. As long as they hang around with the "old gang," there will be pressure—albeit low-key and unspoken—to go along with the crowd. The old friends may even know they are trying to break the addictions. But the need for acceptance will often lead these people to give in, with tragic consequences.

What Am I Worth?

Another need that gets easily twisted is our desire for significance, for feeling that we're somehow important in the world. This need seems especially strong in men. In our culture, significance is usually measured by the type of job you have and how much money and possessions you own. This is a big part of why a man like Ivan Boesky, who already had more money than he could possibly need, continued to use illegal means to make even more millions.

On the level where most of us live, the search for significance often becomes painfully obvious when men get in debt over their heads because they feel compelled to buy boats, cars, fancy houses and other luxuries they can't really afford. Sometimes they lose everything when foolhardy investments go sour, instead of giving them quick wealth.

A financial advisor tells of a former client who retired from a large corporation with a comfortable nest egg. But this retiree had always based his sense of self-worth on his ability to make money, and he felt an ongoing need to prove himself. So he made some risky real estate investments using lots of borrowed money. When the economy in his area turned bad, so did his business deals, and he soon found himself on the verge of bankruptcy.[4]

Many men also equate self-worth with their attractiveness to women. Television and the movies constantly promote the idea that a man who's really a man, who's worth imitating, is one who can seduce beautiful women at the drop of a hat, like James Bond, the fictional spy. Tragically, in real life the result is often men who get involved in extramarital affairs trying to prove they "measure up" in this area.

Am I Secure?

Yet another need that's almost the opposite of significance is the need for security. Rather than wanting to make dangerous investments for quick profits, people driven by a need for security become addicted to behaviors that they think will make them safer. Men who grew up poor or who have lost jobs in the past, for example, may act like workaholics as they try to make themselves indispensable to their employers. Women who equate security with a nice home may spend their families deeply into debt as they continually shop for furnishings and decorations.

I once heard of a woman just like that. She grew up with strong feelings of insecurity, and in her mind, as she interpreted the circumstances of her childhood, she concluded that the key to security was a nice, well-appointed home—something she had never enjoyed. If she could get that, she was sure she would finally have a secure refuge in this world.

Then one day she and her husband inherited a small fortune, and she immediately went out and bought a new house. She became a compulsive shopper as she sought to complete her safe little nest. In just a few short years, the money was gone. And, sadly, she was no more secure than she had been before. In fact, she and her husband were worse off, because the only way they could now maintain the life-style they had adopted was to spend more than their incomes and go into perpetual debt.[5]

Many people these days seem to equate security with physical fitness. Our society puts such a premium on looking young and fit that folks tend to think they have to look forever twenty-five if they're to find or keep a mate, have lots of friends and a happy social life, and get ahead on the job. So they spend millions of dollars each year on diet books, diet foods, diet pills, fitness clubs, exercise equipment, wardrobes full of the latest fashion, face lifts, tummy tucks and liposuction. They're desperate to win the never-ending war against gravity and the natural effects of aging.

Where's the Action?

To different degrees we all need activity and a sense of excitement and fun in our lives. You may not have thought of this as a need before, but we all get bored at times, don't we? When you've been shut up inside for a few days because of illness or bad weather, or when you've just been working hard in an office all week, what do you want to do? You want to get out and move around, maybe take a long hike or find a roller coaster to ride. You want to laugh, to have a little adventure, to enjoy a good time.

This is one big reason people go to amusement parks and adventuresome movies, buy motorcycles and dune buggies, go hang gliding or parachuting or scuba diving—or bet their money at places like horse tracks and gambling casinos. People can actually grow deeply addicted to thrill-seeking, to risk-taking, to "living on the edge." Gamblers also tend to be attracted to the glamour and "fast life" of casinos and race tracks. They really believe the commercials that tell us Las Vegas offers "the American way to play."

The Role of Sin

Unfortunately, when illegitimate ways of getting our needs met present themselves, our human tendency is to go right after them. This is because, as descendants of Adam and Eve, we're sinners by nature.

As we saw in the last chapter, the apostle Paul, speaking about his own struggles with sin, said that even though he wanted to do good, he often did evil instead. Guided by the Holy Spirit, he came to this conclusion: "I find then a law, that evil is present with me, the one who wills to do good. For I delight in the law of God according to the inward man. But I see another law in my members, warring against the law of my mind, and bringing me into captivity to the law of sin which is in my members" (Rom. 7:21-23).

This law of sin, or sinful nature, draws us toward the illicit offer. It makes us want to say yes to temptation. It urges us to believe the lies we hear about how to satisfy our needs for love, security and so on. And even though as Christians we're not supposed to give in to the sin nature—and don't *have* to, either (more about that later)—all too often that's exactly what we do.

Our allowing the sin nature to control us has two ongoing and very negative consequences in terms of our relationship to compulsive desires. First, we lack the spiritual discipline that would help us overcome them. One of the obvious ways to gain the victory over sin in our lives is to spend time with God through prayer and the study of His Word. The psalmist wrote wisely, "How can a young man cleanse his way? By taking heed according to Your word....Your word have I hidden in my heart, that I might not sin against You" (Ps. 119:9,11).

Hiding God's Word in the heart means studying it, memorizing it, meditating on it and thinking through how it applies in the everyday decisions of our lives. If we did those things regularly, we'd see a huge improvement in our lives, and we all know that. Yet how many of us have a daily devotional time? How many of us are memorizing Scripture every week? How many of us have any idea how to meditate on biblical passages so that they become a permanent part of our lives?

Why don't we do these things? There are plenty of books and tapes and other helps to show us how to do them, so lack of knowledge is not the problem. No, the simple fact is that we lack discipline. We're lazy. There are so many other things we'd rather do. It's hard for us to admit God's Word isn't really very important to us, but we all find time—or make time—to do the things we want most to do. Whether it's our jobs, TV, fishing, sports, time with friends, a hobby or something else, we give them priority over attention to God's Word. And so our lack of discipline leaves us weak and vulnerable to compulsive desires.

Second, being controlled by the sin nature means we're seldom content with what we have, and that really sets us up to be dominated by compulsive desires. Compulsive shoppers and overspenders, for example, spurred on by the constant barrage of advertising in our society, are always rushing out to buy the latest fashions, the newest model, the most-advanced gadget.

Last year's clothes, still in good shape, are outdated. Last year's car, still running fine, isn't as sharp as the one fresh off the assembly line. The computer bought two years ago and still doing its job perfectly doesn't operate quite as fast as the model arriving in stores today. So things that have years of useful service left in them are set aside, thrown out or given away while debt is used to buy the new and improved.

"Godliness with contentment is great gain....And having food and clothing, with these we shall be content," Paul said in 1 Timothy 6:6,8. But most of us are far from that attitude. And to the many who are trapped in a compulsive desire for the things of this

40

world, Paul must seem to be speaking a foreign language.

Extramarital affairs are usually fueled by a discontent with one's spouse. Perhaps the marriage has grown a little stale, and maybe the partners are taking each other for granted. So the need for intimacy isn't being met fully, discontentment grows, and the sight of singles who are "free" or couples who seem to have a warm relationship adds to the dissatisfaction. The grass definitely begins to look greener on the other side of the fence.

Then along comes another person, perhaps at the office, who's always well-groomed and nicely dressed. This person is sympathetic, understanding and easy to talk to. Whereas the spouse seems only to nag, this person shows appreciation and clearly enjoys your company. The attractiveness of the spouse pales considerably by comparison.

After a while, the suggestion is made to meet outside the office, maybe over dinner. Before long, new affections have been set, and a physical relationship becomes almost inevitable. The lady quoted in chapter 1 broke off her extramarital relationship just before it got to this stage, but all too often, neither one has the wisdom or self-control to do that. The result is predictable tragedy.

In a similar way an addiction to pornography can be fueled by discontent. Although many men get hooked as teens, such an addiction can also start after marriage. Our culture today teaches that, even after you're married, it's OK to "window shop." In addition, the initial passion of the courtship and honeymoon period inevitably fades, and then a couple settles into the routines of married life. Over the years the husband and wife put on a few pounds and inches, and they also begin to take each other for granted. And everywhere he turns in our "liberated" age, the man sees beautiful, young women who aren't shy about displaying their physical charms.

Once a man in that situation picks up one out of the flood of magazines and videos that are available, he can be on his way to a full-fledged addiction. Not everyone who picks up a *Playboy* will become addicted to pornography, of course. But some will, and every addiction begins with a first experience.

"Rejoice with the wife of your youth," Solomon wrote in the book of Proverbs. "As a loving deer and a graceful doe, let her breasts satisfy you at all times; and always be enraptured with her love" (Prov. 5:18-19). That was sound advice in his day thousands of years ago, and it's equally sound today. Failure to follow it—allowing himself to grow discontented with his wife—can open the door of a man's heart to a compulsive desire for pornography.

Satan, the Devouring Lion

As if the sin nature's corruption of our needs weren't enough to lead us into compulsive desire, we must also deal with an enemy who is out to destroy our souls. I'm speaking, of course, of Satan, the archenemy of God, who is destined for an eternity in hell and wants to take as many people with him as he can. The apostle Peter warned us to "be sober, be vigilant; because your adversary the devil walks about like a roaring lion, seeking whom he may devour" (1 Pet. 5:8).

We may be sure that every time we're tempted to satisfy a legitimate need in an illegitimate way, one of Satan's angels is cheering us on, urging us to make that choice.

And how do the devil and his minions work? After all, if most people knew he was behind their struggles—especially we Christians—they'd surely run away from him. Satan knows that, and he's clever enough to work around our natural and justified revulsion toward him.

Think back to Satan's temptation of Adam and Eve in the Garden of Eden. Did he try to order them to sin? No. Did he warn them that if they disobeyed God they would break their fellowship with God, make their own lives immeasurably harder, and bring down a curse on the whole human race? Of course not. He *deceived* them. He lied. He led them to think God was withholding something good by denying them the fruit of that one tree, to believe they would be better off if they did what God had clearly told them not to. And they bought the lie.

Jesus said of Satan that he "does not stand in the truth, because there is no truth in him. When he speaks a lie, he speaks from his own resources, for he is a liar and the father of it" (John 8:44). The apostle Paul wrote of him, "For Satan...transforms himself into an angel of light. Therefore it is no great thing if his ministers also transform themselves into ministers of righteousness'' (2 Cor. 11:14-15).

When it comes to obeying God and doing what's right, living free of sinful compulsive desires, the devil and his minions will try to convince us that bad is good, that black is white, that a wrong act can be justified to the Lord's satisfaction. They're all lies, but he's the consummate liar. He ought to be the best—he's been doing it since before the creation of the world (see 1 John 3:8).

''At every fork in the road,'' a wise man once said, ''the devil is dangling the carrot down the wrong path.'' He'll make that carrot seem like the most tasty bit of food in the universe, but the path he'll take us on to get it leads to hell, not heaven.

Understand, too, that Satan knows us all too well. He knows our needs—he's been observing human nature since the time of Adam and Eve. And he looks inside us and sees which of our needs are weak spots, which ones aren't being met and haven't been submitted to the lordship of Jesus Christ. If we have areas like that in our lives, *we can be sure he'll find them out and tempt us in exactly those places*.

Two recent novels, *This Present Darkness* and *Piercing the Darkness* by Frank Peretti, have been extremely popular, largely because they show how Satan and his demons attack and control people in this day and age. Although the novels reflect the imagination of only one Christian writer and are not Scripture, they nonetheless make the reality of demons and spiritual warfare graphically clear. Satan is alive and active in our world, trying to deceive and destroy everyone he can. Don't let him fool you into thinking otherwise.

Like a doctor diagnosing a patient's illness, we need to understand the problem before we can go on to prescribe the proper medicine. And we've seen now *why* compulsive desires are able to enslave us. Next we'll look at another part of the picture, which is *how* they do it.

FOUR

HOW OUR DESIRES CONTROL US

A young Christian woman indicated a genuine desire to live for the Lord. She kept an honest, upright life-style. But then on one fateful occasion she yielded to temptation and engaged in sexual sin. Afterward, she was consumed with guilt and the understanding that she could never regain her virginity.

As a believer did she then confess her sin to God, repent of it and accept His cleansing, as we're instructed to do in 1 John 1:9? Would that she had! Instead, tricked by Satan's lie into thinking a fresh start was forever denied her, she threw aside all caution and gave herself over to sexual promiscuity with a multitude of men. When she became pregnant as a result, she couldn't even say for sure who the father was.[1]

Done in by Deceit

That poor girl's experience illustrates two of the ways in which even God's children can be controlled by sinful compulsive desires. First, we're deceived by the devil into believing falsehoods. Our enemy is able to "pull the wool over our eyes," just as he did with Adam and Eve and has been doing ever since.

In the case of the young woman above, he was able to convince her that God was not her loving heavenly Father but only a stern, unforgiving judge. Despite all the clear biblical evidence to the contrary, she accepted the lie that her sin was too terrible for God to forgive.

Solomon, in the book of Proverbs, personified foolishness as a woman and put these words in her mouth: " 'Whoever is simple [naive], let him turn in here'; and as for him who lacks understanding, she says to him, 'Stolen water is sweet, and bread eaten in secret is pleasant.' But he does not know that the dead are there, and her guests are in the depths of hell" (9:16-18).

Unfortunately, far too many Christians are naive enough to fall for such lies, to believe that stolen things are better than those gained honestly, that illicit pleasures are more enjoyable than the pure. The recovering alcoholic will buy the lie that "just one little drink'' will do no harm. The man addicted to lust will believe that he can ''handle'' just one X-rated movie without falling back into the habit. The gambler will accept the notion that one small bet is no big deal. The cocaine addict who's trying to kick the drug will insist there's nothing wrong with staying close to old, still-addicted friends.

Truly, the human capacity to be deceived—even among Christians—seems almost limitless. Satan knows this and spins his lies with great skill.

Ruled by the Past

The second means of control demonstrated in our opening story is a particularly effective lie of the devil: the belief that having once fallen in sin we're doomed to repeat the failure forever after. The tendency here is to think we're ruled by the past. As our failure has been, so must it always be.

Satan works in this case with the tremendous guilt we naturally feel after we sin. We get discouraged, we see ourselves as failures, we conclude we're unable to stand up for God, and we resign ourselves to sinning again in the same way. When that self-prophecy is fulfilled, our negative assessment of ourselves and our ability to resist temptation is confirmed and made all the stronger. Then it really does get easier to sin each time thereafter.

As an insightful writer has said, ''Sins multiply in the soil of discouragement. One offense easily leads to another. You are caught in a vicious circle until you realize that your past need not control your future."[2]

Unresolved guilt, besides setting us up to repeat the sin, has other negative consequences as well. It can cause physical illness. Worry over being found out can lead to stomach ailments. The strain of trying to forget or deny past sins can cause the body to break down. Some doctors suggest that almost half their patients could be healed if they could just believe they've been forgiven.

Guilt also contributes to a lack of faith in God. It's hard to trust Him when we expect Him to "drop the ax" on us at any time for what we've done.

Some people punish themselves, mentally or even physically, in a futile effort to atone for their sins. They believe they must pay a penalty for their failures, and in effect they refuse to accept Jesus' sacrifice on their behalf. Others go in the opposite direction, doing good works in an attempt to appease God. They feel that if they give away their time, money and efforts to help others, God will take notice and figure they've balanced the books.[3]

Of course, God's grace doesn't work that way. Jesus has already atoned for our sins and balanced the books, as the Bible makes so clear. But many Christians go right on trying to do it all themselves, motivated by their unresolved guilt.

Puffed Up With Pride

A third way we're controlled by compulsive desires

is just the opposite of being ruled by the past. (Satan is extremely inventive in leading us astray and can work with our individual tendencies whatever they may be.) Some of us get puffed up with pride, thinking we've got our sinful habits licked and under control. We don't need to struggle or be on guard anymore. All is well.

As the Bible says so clearly and simply, however, "Pride goes before destruction, and a haughty spirit before a fall" (Prov. 16:18). The time when we think we've got a sinful habit beaten is the time when we're most vulnerable to falling again.

A recovering alcoholic who studied his problem found that when alcoholics start to get straightened out, they begin to take pride in their sobriety. They feel better physically and may regain jobs and the respect of family members. They say things like, "You know, I haven't had a drink in a month now, and I'm never going to let my life get messed up like that again." Then they develop a superior attitude toward friends who drink.

After a while they conclude they've solved the problems that led to their addiction and have the situation under control. All this time, old friends have been offering them drinks, and they've refused. But now, when a buddy suggests, "You can handle it," they're ready to believe they really can. Surely just one drink will be OK. And in saying yes, they doom themselves to falling under the rule of alcohol once again, because the fact is alcoholics *can't* "handle" even one drink.[4]

Unfortunately, that cycle alcoholics go through is typical of us all regardless of the specific problem with which we struggle. Whether it's pornography or gambling or compulsive eating or whatever, pride tends to follow right on the heels of our first successes in resisting temptation. It's so easy, after staying straight for just a few weeks, to think we've won the war and will never fall again. But when we do, we're actually just about to step into the enemy's most deadly ambush.

Worn Down by Temptation

Have you ever noticed how you can say no to a temptation of the mind—pride or envy or lust, for example—and ten seconds later you're being assaulted again by the exact same temptation? We can be entirely sincere in our desire to say no to a compulsive desire. We can ask for God's help, walk away from the source of temptation, do whatever it takes to resist the desire. And yet no sooner is the victory won than we're staring the very same desire squarely in the face once again.

"Temptations, unlike opportunities, will always give you a second chance," someone once said with great wisdom. All our best and most sincere efforts won't banish a compulsive desire forever. The corrupted human nature is all too quick to jump at a second chance to indulge in sin. And in our culture, temptation is almost impossible to avoid.

Relatively speaking, a first temptation to, say, envy

52

can be easy to resist. But then you look out your living room window and see your neighbor driving his new car into his garage. That makes you think of the expensive repairs you're facing on your eight-year-old rolling wreck, and the envy begins.

You pray and then decide to get your mind onto something else, so you pick up your weekly news magazine. Flipping it open, you're confronted by a full-page, full-color ad for your dream car.

Throwing the magazine onto the coffee table, you walk over and turn on the TV. You're just in time to see a lady win a new Cadillac on "The Price Is Right." Switching channels in disgust, you find yourself looking at "Lifestyles of the Rich and Famous" and some Hollywood star driving along the coast in an expensive European car.

By now, envy isn't nearly so easy to resist as it was the first time around. As we struggle with the same compulsive desire over and over, it gets harder and harder to hold out. Giving in—the course of least resistance—seems to make more and more sense. We can get just plain worn down by the constant struggle.

This is why the apostle Paul encouraged us in Galatians 6:9, "And let us not grow weary while doing good, for in due season we shall reap [everlasting life] if we do not lose heart." But when we're alone and facing the same temptation for the twentieth time that day, it's so easy to grow weary and lose heart.

Burned by Fire

In the previous section I talked about the persistence of temptation in spite of our sincere wish to resist it. But the painful truth is that many times we're not nearly so eager to be rid of it. We want to play with it in our minds, to fantasize, to entertain "What if…" thoughts and imaginings. We're like foolishly curious children playing with matches. We don't want to get burned, but we surely do want a good, close look at the fire. As A.W. Tozer said, "No Christian ever fell into sin who did not first allow himself to brood over it with increasing desire."

Think back to the fall of the great king David into sin with Bathsheba. How did it happen? The Bible says one evening, "David arose from his bed and walked on the roof of the king's house. And from the roof he saw a woman bathing, and the woman was very beautiful to behold" (2 Sam. 11:2). He saw this beautiful woman, and he was tempted.

Now it's not surprising that a man who sees an attractive woman in the nude would become aroused. And God had given David a wife for the proper and healthy satisfaction of his sexual needs. In fact, David had a number of wives by that time, any one of whom would have spent the night with him gladly. He knew that. Yet he allowed his mind to dwell on the woman he had seen. He couldn't or wouldn't turn his thoughts into sanctified channels.

Brooding over the woman led David next to send for information about her. This produced news that should have stopped him dead in his sinful tracks several times over.

First, she was a married woman. This alone should have caused him to do whatever was necessary to put her out of his mind once and for all, for God had spoken clearly to Moses in the Ten Commandments, "You shall not covet your neighbor's wife" (Ex. 20:17). To disobey that command meant earning the just wrath of God—there could have been no doubt about that in David's mind. And who knew what such disobedience on the part of the king, who was to set the example for all Israel, could cost him and the nation?

Second, she was the wife of Uriah the Hittite, a man listed in 2 Samuel 23:39 as one of David's "mighty men"—his most courageous and effective warriors. Uriah had served David faithfully, at the risk of his life, in many battles, dispatching scores of David's enemies to the grave. For David to take this man's wife was an act of treachery in exchange for Uriah's brave loyalty, and David should have been too ashamed to give the idea further thought. Practically speaking, David should have also realized that such an action would cause *all* his soldiers to ask, "If the king would do that to a servant so great as Uriah, what might he do to the rest of us?"

So spiritually and ethically and just in terms of being a wise leader, David had every reason to rein in his heart and forget Bathsheba. But by this time his thoughts were consumed with her. His burning, lustful desire was all that mattered. Love of God, fear of the Lord, respect for a faithful soldier, honor for a married woman, common sense—David was beyond all these. He would have the woman whatever the cost. And so he made the decision that would cost untold innocent lives and tear apart his family.

Believe me, there's no such thing as an idle thought. We are what we think. Nothing reveals our true selves as much as the things we allow our minds to dwell on habitually. And those things will inevitably show up in our attitudes, our words and our actions. This is why Paul urged us to be "bringing *every* thought into captivity to the obedience of Christ" (2 Cor. 10:5, my emphasis).

Felled in Stages

Notice, too, that David fell into sin in stages. It didn't happen all at once but over time in several steps that led him steadily away from God and into disaster. And so it will usually be with us as well.

First he saw Bathsheba bathing. It was at night, on his rooftop, and he may well have been alone. He probably lingered over the sight, and lust was conceived.

Then he chose to let his mind brood over the sight of her, as I discussed in the preceding section. He filled his mind with her image rather than channel his thoughts properly.

Next he sought information about her. Now he was revealing his thoughts to others and beginning to put his sinful desires into action.

After that he sent messengers to fetch Bathsheba. His sinful intentions were obvious to all concerned, and others who should have been serving God were being required to aid their lecherous king in satisfying his lust. As we would say in modern terminology, they were being made accessories to the crime.

Even at this point, however, with Bathsheba in front of him in his chambers, David could have come to his senses and sent her away without taking her to bed. But overcome with desire, he chose to sleep with her in violation of God's commandment and every law of human decency.

Later, when Bathsheba sent word that he had impregnated her, David took the further step of bringing her husband home from battle in the hope that Uriah would sleep with his wife and so be deceived into thinking the child to be born was his. Like a train racing downhill out of control, David's list of sins was charging ahead: lust, enlisting partners in crime, treachery against a loyal servant, adultery and now deceit.

When Uriah proved himself a better man than the king, refusing the comforts of his wife's bed while his comrades were still away at war, David took the next sinful step of ordering Uriah's murder. That way, the man would never be able to accuse his king of adultery, and David would be free to marry Bathsheba. And so what had begun as lustful passion ended in a cold-blooded decision to kill an innocent man.

Likewise impetuous Simon Peter, who denied the

Lord Jesus on the night of His betrayal, fell to that low point in stages as he was led astray by Satan. During the Last Supper, Jesus had told Peter, "Simon, Simon! Indeed, Satan has asked for you, that he may sift you as wheat. But I have prayed for you, that your faith should not fail" (Luke 22:31-32).

As pointed out earlier, Satan is well aware of those areas of our lives that are uncommitted to God, and he will tempt us in exactly those places. In Peter's case his weakness was in his understanding of who Jesus was. Peter had left everything behind—his family, his work, his friends—to follow Jesus because he believed Him to be the promised Messiah. To that extent he was correct. But he was convinced the Messiah had to be a political leader who would throw out the hated Roman rulers and occupiers of Israel. He refused to accept the truth Jesus taught that He had come not to overturn political empires but to die on a cross and so save people from their sins.

On the night of Jesus' betrayal, just before He warned Peter that Satan wanted to sift him, the disciples had been arguing among themselves over which of them was the greatest. They were still anticipating the establishment of Jesus' earthly kingdom and were dividing up the positions of power and honor ahead of time. No doubt Peter was a part of this argument.

Later, Peter was one of the three disciples Jesus took with Him to the inner part of the Garden of Gethsemane to be nearest Him while He prayed. There He gave them the instruction, "Pray that you may not enter into temptation'' (Luke 22:40). Then He went a short distance away and prayed in such agony that He sweat blood.

How did Peter respond to Jesus' warning and instruction? Did he keep watch and pray in that decisive hour, knowing he would be tested? No, he (along with the others) promptly fell asleep! When Jesus came back He directly rebuked Peter, ''What, could you not watch with Me one hour? Watch and pray, lest you enter into temptation'' (Matt. 26:40-41). And a second time Peter dropped off to sleep. A vital opportunity for spiritual strengthening had been tossed aside.

The next step down Peter's path to denial came when the soldiers arrived with Judas to arrest Jesus. Still thinking Jesus had to overthrow Roman rule and being unprepared spiritually, Peter drew a sword and tried to hack off the head of a member of the arresting party. Once again Jesus had to rebuke him, saying, ''Put your sword into the sheath. Shall I not drink the cup which My Father has given Me?'' (John 18:11).

Now more confused and frightened than ever, Peter followed the arresting party to the high priest's house. And there, as the culmination of his steps away from the Lord, Peter denied his Savior three times, just as Jesus had predicted. Only when the rooster crowed, as Jesus had also foretold, did Peter realize what he had done.

In the same way our falling into addiction to compulsive desires will usually take place through a series of steps. If we were confronted right at the start with the enormity of the sins we would commit, we might be appalled and run to God for help to stay pure. But instead we're led away one step, one decision, one compromise at a time, often not realizing what we've done until we're hooked—if even then.

Doomed by Going It Alone

Have you ever known someone who was too proud, too stubborn, too blind or just too stupid to ask for help, even though help was available? Almost certainly you have, because the unwillingness to ask for help is a common human trait. You may well be such a person yourself.

When this trait is carried over into spiritual matters, it becomes one of the principal means by which compulsive desires control us. Through pride, ignorance or fear of God, we keep our distance from Him and try to solve all our problems on our own, including our struggles with addictions of whatever kind. Satan is well aware of this tendency and works continually to keep us trying to make it by ourselves.

Knowing how much people like to "make it on their own" and "pull themselves up by their own bootstraps," and knowing how Satan would use that tendency to keep us enslaved, God saw to it that a number of clear teachings about the matter were included in His Word.

In John 15, for example, Jesus uses a beautiful word picture to explain our need for Him if we're to resist temptation and serve Him. "I am the true vine," He said, "and My Father is the vinedresser....Abide in Me, and I in you. As the branch cannot bear fruit of itself, unless it abides in the vine, neither can you, unless you abide in Me. I am the vine, you are the branches. He who abides in Me, and I in him, bears much fruit; *for without Me you can do nothing*" (vv. 1,4-5, my emphasis).

The fact is that we can't make it on our own. We need the Lord's strength and wisdom. (Just how we draw on them is the subject of the second part of this book.) Truly, apart from Him there can be no spiritual victory. Anything we hear to the contrary is a lie.

The Lord knew the people of Israel needed such a warning way back in the time of Moses. As they were preparing to enter the promised land and claim it as their own, He knew they would tend to grow self-sufficient, forgetting who had really provided their success and prosperity. So He instructed them through Moses, "Beware that you do not forget the Lord your God by not keeping His command-ments...lest—when you have eaten and are full, and have built beautiful houses and dwell in them...and all that you have is multiplied...—then you say in your heart, 'My power and the might of my hand have gained me this wealth' " (Deut. 8:11-13,17).

Taken to the extreme, the attitude that says we can make it on our own denies our need of a Savior. But the truth is that just as we can't possibly save our-selves, so also we can't live holy lives apart from abiding in Him. We are dependent people, and the

61

more we're willing to admit that, the more He's able to help us overcome compulsive desires.

A woman named Mary illustrates the futility of going it alone. Her compulsive desire was for food, but she was confident she could eat properly and lose weight whenever she really made up her mind to do it. Gaining a few extra pounds made her feel guilty, however, and she responded by resolving to stick to her diet. She determined she would *never* overeat again.

You can guess what happened. Her self-control failed repeatedly, which made her feel more and more guilty. Eventually she gave up even trying to control her gluttony. Said the pastor who first told Mary's story, "I've discovered that promises to reform are not only worthless, but even detrimental in changing our behavior. One reason is [that] we are depending on our own strength to change. Even when we ask God to help us keep that promise, we have as yet not grasped the extent of our weakness."[5]

As long as we hang on to the false notion that we can overcome compulsive desires on our own, we're doomed to failure.

Focused on the Wrong Places

Yet another way we're controlled by our desires is that our focus is often stuck on problems that seem serious enough in and of themselves, yet they're only symptoms of more serious, underlying concerns.

One day a man called his pastor and asked for help

of a very practical nature. It seemed the man could not force himself to get to work on time, and he had lost several previous jobs due to his laziness. Could the pastor help him develop his willpower? The pastor made some suggestions he hoped would be of value.

A week later, the pastor learned this man was involved in an illicit sexual affair. The lack of self-control that had led him to give free rein to his lust was affecting every area of his life. Yet he was focusing on the superficial problem of tardiness in reporting to work. The underlying lust that controlled him was closed to inspection.[6]

As long as our focus stays on the superficial and we fail to get at our root problems, our compulsive desires will remain in control.

Stuck in Our Comfort Zones

Psychologists and social workers have discovered an interesting phenomenon: women and children in abusive homes will often choose to remain in those homes rather than be removed to foster homes, shelters or other places of safety—even though they know staying means suffering further abuse. Why? Because as painful as their home situations may be, those places are familiar. They know what to expect there, and they think they've learned to survive in one way or another. Any other situation, on the other hand, is strange and represents change and having to start over.

In the same way we may resist giving up our

compulsive desires even though we know they're sinful and make us feel guilty—simply because we've grown accustomed to them, and freedom from them would be a major change in our lives. Our attitude seems to be, "It may be a sinful compulsive desire, but it's my addiction. And if I give it up, who can say what my life will become? It might even get worse. At least now I know what to expect each day."

It's a perverse sort of reasoning, and it takes place mostly at a subconscious level. But it's a very real mindset that afflicts many people and keeps them halfhearted at best in their efforts to overcome controlling sinful desires. And as the apostle James pointed out, double-minded people are unstable in all their ways and can expect nothing but spiritual failure (see James 1:6-8).

As we've seen, Satan and the sinful nature have many powerful tools with which to keep us enslaved to our compulsive desires. Victory comes only at the expense of continual vigilance and struggle. But this raises a question: why is freedom so hard to gain? Why doesn't a loving, all-powerful God just take away our sinful addictions and give us freedom? We'll consider that crucial question next.

FIVE

WHY DOESN'T GOD FREE US INSTANTLY?

Sometime after God destroyed Sodom and Gomorrah with fire and brimstone, Abraham journeyed south and stayed for a while in a land known as Gerar. And just as he had earlier in Egypt, Abraham feared that if the men there knew the beautiful Sarah was his wife they would kill him in order to get her. So he instructed Sarah to tell everyone she was only his sister.

When they arrived in Gerar, the men did indeed notice Sarah's beauty, and word of her soon got to the king, Abimelech. He promptly sent for her, intending to take her as his wife (one of many, no doubt). The stage was set for adultery and God's judgment on all concerned.

But God intervened. He didn't let it happen. He stepped into the scene in a most direct and unmistakable way, appearing to Abimelech in a dream. "Indeed you are a dead man because of the woman whom you have taken," He told the king, "for she is a man's wife" (Gen. 20:3).

Abimelech, who had not yet touched Sarah and who was apparently a God-fearing man, answered back, "Lord, will You slay a righteous nation also? Did he [Abraham] not say to me, 'She is my sister'? And she, even she herself said, 'He is my brother.' In the integrity of my heart and innocence of my hands I have done this" (vv. 4-5).

Now read closely God's response: "Yes, I know that you did this in the integrity of your heart. *For I also withheld you from sinning against Me; therefore I did not let you touch her*" (v. 6, my emphasis).

Whether Abimelech had a particular compulsive desire for women we don't know, but my point here is that he was about to do something sinful—take another man's wife as his own—and God stopped him. Somehow He kept him from touching Sarah prior to the dream conversation. This was a direct action of the Lord. And then He appeared to him and gave him the information quoted above. So in two ways, at two different times, God made sure Abimelech did not sin with Sarah.

This story is unusual, to be sure. But it shouldn't surprise us that God is able to do that sort of thing if He so chooses. He's an all-knowing, all-powerful God. He can do anything He wants, including keep us human beings from sinning. The big question is why He doesn't choose to do it more often.

When we're struggling with compulsive desires, wouldn't our lives be a lot easier and more pleasant if God would just take away the desires or at least put insurmountable roadblocks in our way when we're about to give in to temptation? Wouldn't that spare us a lot of misery and guilt? So why doesn't our loving heavenly Father intervene in our lives the way He did in Abimelech's in Genesis 20? I think all of us have asked that kind of question at one time or another, and in this chapter we need to consider some answers.

Adam's Children

One part of why God doesn't usually free us from the struggle relates to our being descendants of Adam. Beginning with that first man, God gave us free will. Just as He chose to love us despite our sinfulness, so He wants us to choose to love and obey Him. He doesn't want us to be robots who love Him only because we have no choice or are afraid of Him— that wouldn't really be love at all, would it? No, He wants us to respond to His love by freely loving Him in return. As the apostle John said, "There is no fear in love; but perfect love casts out fear....We love Him because He first loved us" (1 John 4:18-19).

Unfortunately, Adam and Eve exercised their free will by choosing to disobey the Lord and eat the fruit of the forbidden tree, and all their descendants have inherited their sinful nature. As a result, we're all constantly choosing to sin in so many ways, including giving in to our compulsive desires. And God is still seeking not robots, but people who will love Him of their own accord. (See Ps. 100 for a beautiful example of the heart's attitude He seeks.) So He's still asking for our love and obedience, not taking away our freedom to decide in times of temptation.

A statement I found puts this fact of life in a nutshell: "That person who is no longer tempted has long since been laid permanently to rest! Temptation is part of the price of being human."

Testing Our Loyalty

Since God wants our willing obedience, it naturally follows that He sometimes allows us to be tempted in order to test whether we will in fact be loyal to Him. After all, it's easy for us to *say* we love Him and will always be faithful, but we can't *know* that for sure, and we can't prove it to Him, until we're actually tempted and have to choose how we'll respond. (Note that God does not tempt us to sin; see James 1:13-14. But He does allow temptation from Satan and the world to come into our lives.)

We see a clear example of God's testing in the story of Hezekiah, one of the good kings of Judah after Israel was divided following Solomon's death. Hezekiah did much to lead his people back to the worship of the Lord after years of backsliding. God was with him and blessed him in all he did. On one occasion, however, He put Hezekiah's loyalty and humility to the test.

The king had been deathly ill—indeed, only God's miraculous intervention spared him (see 2 Kin. 20:1-11). Partly out of concern for Hezekiah, and partly out of curiosity because of hearing about all Hezekiah had accomplished, the king of Babylon sent ambassadors to him with a present and a get-well letter. And the Bible says that when they came, ''God withdrew from him [Hezekiah], in order to test him, that He might know all that was in his heart'' (2 Chr. 32:31).

Whereas God had been with him in the past, guiding him into wise decisions, now He withdrew the Spirit so He could see how Hezekiah would act on his own. Would he act wisely toward these emissaries from a pagan, violent land? Would he be humble and give God the glory for what He had done through him in Judah?

Unfortunately, Hezekiah was arrogant and unwise, showing the Babylonians all the treasures God had given him. What he demonstrated was not humility but pride in what he thought *he* had accomplished. What the Babylonians took home to their king was the news that Judah was a rich land they ought to conquer. And when the prophet Isaiah told Hezekiah that Babylon would come some day to pillage Judah, the king's only response was relief that it wouldn't happen in his lifetime—certainly not godlike concern for his people! (For the whole story, see 2 Kin. 20:12-19).

Just as the Lord so clearly tested Hezekiah on that

occasion, so He also uses temptation to test all that's in our hearts. Nothing shows how much we really trust Him, how much we're committed to obeying His will, as the way we respond to temptation. And each time we're confronted with a sinful compulsive desire, the choice we make demonstrates once again the condition of our hearts.

Our Lord Jesus went through the same kind of testing. Remember the time when He spent forty days and forty nights fasting in the desert, and then Satan came and tempted Him, offering Him the whole world if He would bow down and worship. At the very beginning of that passage we're told, ''Then Jesus was led up by the Spirit into the wilderness to be tempted by the devil'' (Matt. 4:1).

Note first that Jesus was led there by the Holy Spirit. This was no accident, no coincidence that put Jesus and the devil in the same place at the same time. Then notice that the Spirit led Jesus there for the specific purpose of testing Him. Satan didn't manage somehow to sneak up on the Lord while He was trying to do something else. The devil is arrogant enough that he probably thought otherwise—he probably thought *he* had arranged everything. But the heavenly Father, who was preparing His Son for His public ministry, knew He needed to be tested first in a direct confrontation with the enemy.

Jesus passed His test. He met each temptation with Scripture and proved His understanding of the Father's will and His faithfulness to it. Now consider this: if our heavenly Father knew Jesus needed to be tested by temptation, how much more do *we* need such testing?

Conformed to Christ

The fact that Jesus needed to be tested leads directly to the next reason I find for God's allowing us to struggle with our compulsive desires. His primary purpose in helping us to grow as Christians is *not* to make us happy or to keep us comfortable. Instead, He wants most of all to see us become more and more like His Son. And the pain and struggle of wrestling with temptation is one of the best ways for us to grow more like Christ.

Think back over the last few years of your life. When everything has been going well—when everyone in your family was healthy and happy, when there's been more than enough money to pay all the bills—how close have you felt to God? How dependent upon Him did you feel?

Most people, including Christians, tend to feel self-sufficient when life is going well. Oh, we may continue going to church and living piously, and we may even be thankful, but inside we tend to think *we* have everything under control. With a healthy bank balance we don't seem so much in need of God's daily blessings.

But think now of a time when things weren't going so well—when a family member was seriously ill or you were out of a job or a teenager was rebelling. How regular was your prayer life then? How much did you sense a need of God's presence and strength?

Jesus was humble. "He humbled Himself and became obedient to the point of death, even the death of the cross" (Phil. 2:8). Struggling with temptation helps us to stay humble, too. To face the same sinful desire for the tenth time in a half hour makes it abundantly clear that we're far from sainthood.

Jesus was dependent on the Father. He told those persecuting Him, "The Son can do nothing of Himself, but what He sees the Father do....I can of Myself do nothing....I do not seek My own will but the will of the Father who sent Me" (John 5:19,30). We never feel our need of the Father more than when we're struggling against habitual sin. Such times make us painfully aware of how inadequate we are to please Him without His strength and wisdom. Truly, every temptation is an opportunity to draw closer to God in absolute dependence upon Him.

Jesus was incredibly patient. He waited thirty years, laboring as a carpenter until the Father's perfect time, to reveal Himself to humanity as our Savior. He endured the endless pride, ignorance and spiritual blindness of His disciples in order to prepare them, at the end of His time with them, to take the gospel to every corner of the known world. Rather than call down thousands of angels to destroy His enemies, as He easily could have at any time, He allowed Himself to be unjustly tried, beaten, spat upon and executed in order to pay the penalty of our sin and redeem us.

Likewise, if we allow it, our temptations will help

us develop Christlike patience. "My brethren, count it all joy when you fall into various trials," wrote the apostle James, "knowing that the testing of your faith produces patience" (James 1:2-3). This will include patience with ourselves so that we don't give up in despair despite repeated failures, as well as patience with others when they also fall. It will mean patience with God, too, when He doesn't work things out according to the schedule we had expected.

Witness of His Grace

When we let Him, God uses any pain we experience as a testimony to others of His grace and sufficiency. For example, a young woman named Kim trained hard for four years to make the U.S. Olympic team as a speed skater. She was dedicated to her goal and put in long hours on the ice in preparation for the time trials that would determine who represented our country. As a result of all her efforts and God-given talent, she went into those trials as the top-ranked woman in the world in her event.

Unfortunately, on the day of the trials, Kim didn't skate quite as fast as usual, and she missed out on making the team by the tiniest of margins—four hundredths of a second! Naturally she was downhearted, but she also felt the presence and peace of the Lord. And when a woman later asked her how she was able to remain calm in the face of her loss, she replied, "Well, it's because I've given my life to Christ, and He gives me strength."

Because of Kim's witness, the woman who had asked the question gave her life to Christ that very day. Kim had been honest about the pain she felt, but she could also say honestly that He gave her the strength to get through it, and He used that testimony to change an eternal destiny.[1]

What about our struggles with compulsive desires? How can God use them as a witness to His grace? As in Kim's case, it depends on our willingness. If we're the kind of Christians who appear to have no fun in life and are determined that no one else will have fun, either, we'll turn off more people than we attract. But if we can speak honestly of a God who gives us the strength and wisdom to resist temptations to evil—and who still loves us and forgives us when we fail—others will be drawn to Him.

Whole families have been saved because an alcoholic member reported his life had been turned around by God's grace. Countless people have been helped along the path to salvation over the years by Augustine's honest account of his struggles with temptation in his *Confessions*. And the New Testament story that has perhaps drawn as many people to salvation as any other is Jesus' parable of the prodigal son. Here was a young man who apparently had compulsive desires for wine and women, yet knowledge of his father's love eventually turned his heart and his feet toward home, where his forgiving father welcomed him with open arms.

If our struggles with habitual sin only give us the opportunity to tell people how quick our Father is to forgive when we turn back to Him in repentance, they still serve a wonderful purpose. He doesn't want us to live in defeat, of course. But if we're willing, no pain and no defeat are wasted in His economy as we grow in spiritual maturity.

A fellow pastor expressed some beautiful thoughts in this regard, and while he was writing about the value of pain generally, I think his insights apply just as well to the specific pain caused by our struggles against sinful compulsive desires: "I am glad that a loving Father knows there are some things more important than living a life without hurt. Righteousness is more important, and in His love and sovereignty He sometimes allows me to suffer so that I might follow Him more closely. Given the alternative of being without Him, pain is sometimes a gift of His love."[2]

Wounded Healers

Think of the life and ministry of Corrie ten Boom. While a young woman, she saw her family torn apart and sent off to concentration camps by the Nazis because the Ten Booms had dared to protect Jews from the Holocaust. Corrie saw her sister die in one of those camps, and she herself was the victim of much cruelty at the hands of the guards. Yet by God's grace she did not grow embittered and unforgiving. Just the opposite.

After World War II, Corrie had one of the most effective evangelistic outreaches of this century.

Why? Because people knew she was telling the truth when she said, "I've suffered, and I know pain. If anyone has a reason to hate and remain embittered, it's me. Yet God has shown me a better way. By His grace, instead of hating the guards who caused my pain and my sister's death, I've forgiven them and hugged them and led them to the Savior."

Many pastors have been helped by the honest account of the pastor whose struggle with lust I described at the beginning of chapter 3. He isn't completely free of lust even now. But as he has sought, with the Lord's help, to overcome his addiction, he, too, has become a wounded healer. God has used him to give strength and hope to many of His servants.

Wounded healers can help others in many ways. There are times when we simply need to be with people and by our loving presence reassure them of God's love. Knowing we've gone through the same struggles will mean more to them than anything we might say. When we do speak, it will be with an experience-based authority others don't have. And in those times when we need to hold people accountable for their actions, they'll know we're admonishing them because we found it necessary in our own battles with habitual sin.

As we think about the ministry we can have as wounded healers to fellow strugglers, I can't help thinking again about our Lord Jesus, who suffered unjustly but without complaint for our sakes. And one of the most comforting passages I find in the entire Bible is this: "For we do not have a High Priest who cannot sympathize with our weaknesses, but was in all points tempted as we are, yet without sin. Let us therefore come boldly to the throne of grace, that we may obtain mercy and find grace to help in time of need'' (Heb. 4:15-16).

Truly, He is the greatest of wounded healers. As we battle our compulsive desires, He knows exactly what we're going through. And when we fail, He's standing at the throne of grace, ready to give mercy and grace to help in our time of need. Let us therefore draw near with boldness.

SIX

EMOTIONS:
HELP OR
HINDRANCE?

George is a compulsive overeater, and he knows it. He's especially aware of it when he steps on the bathroom scales in the morning. Although he's always dieting—or so he tells himself—he never loses more than a few pounds. And then he puts them back on again within the next week or two.

This is how George's typical day goes: when he stands on the scales and sees he hasn't lost anything or has even gained a little, he gets upset with himself. The scales remind him in no uncertain terms that he's been overeating again. "All right," he tells himself, "I've got to get serious about my diet. No cheating today!" He's frustrated but determined. Like a football player about to dash onto the field at the start of a game, he's "charged up" emotionally, ready to take on the enemy—excess calories—and win.

Resolved to lose weight, he eats a small breakfast—maybe even skips it. When coworkers offer him a donut at the morning break, he declines and sticks to his coffee, feeling proud of himself. When friends invite him to join them for lunch, he again says no and eats the low-calorie lunch his wife has prepared.

By the time afternoon break rolls around, however, the emotions and determination of the early morning are fading away. Besides, the small breakfast and lunch have left him hungry. Now it seems as though the Almond Joy candy bars (George's favorite) in the lunchroom vending machines are calling out to him, "Here we are, George, just waiting for you! Eat us! Eat us!"

"I really *am* hungry," George tells himself. "And I've been good today. I didn't eat nearly as much for lunch as I normally would. So one candy bar shouldn't hurt me all that much. Besides, it's got almonds in it, and they're nutritious." After a few more minutes of rationalizing his decision, he heads off for the vending machine.

That night at home, George eats a full, satisfying, healthy dinner then parks in front of the TV for the evening. And after the late news, when the rest of the family has gone to bed, he starts feeling hungry again. I wonder what there is in the kitchen to snack on, he says to himself. The emotions and resolve of the morning have been completely forgotten as he rummages through the refrigerator for some tasty leftovers. As he plops into his chair at the dining room table, a fried drumstick in one hand and a bag of potato chips in the other, he glances at his watch and tells himself, No wonder I'm hungry! It's been four hours since supper!

Ruled by Feelings

Like so many people today, George is ruled by his feelings. In the morning, staring at the scales, he gets emotionally cranked up for dieting. He's been reminded of just how heavy he is. He thinks of the clothes that don't fit anymore. He does a quick mental calculation of how far he is over his "ideal" weight. And his mind flashes ahead to his tennis match with Hank later in the week and how he's going to feel like an elephant as he lumbers from side to side on the tennis court.

At that point in the morning, you could probably put a gun to George's head, and he still wouldn't eat a donut. But he doesn't stay at that level of emotion very long. No one does. Over the next few hours, the feelings of upset and determination fade. As he gets into the routine of the day, his emotions also fall into their normal pattern. Then the habits that go with his addiction to overeating re-emerge and take control once again. By the time the day is done, his feelings have gone from "I'll never eat another bite!" to "I deserve a break today!"

George's story illustrates one of the major problems with being ruled by our feelings: they go up and down all the time, depending on our circumstances. Our emotions react naturally to our experiences. And if how we respond is determined by what we feel, our behavior will show the same lack of consistency. What we know to be right—and all our good intentions to walk the straight and narrow way—will be at the mercy of the passions of the moment.

James Dobson tells a good story that shows how emotions can overrule our reason. Back in 1969, after the Charles Manson "family" had committed its terrible murders, people all over the Los Angeles area were living in great fear, wondering if they might be the next victims. Among those engulfed in the wave of terror were Dobson's elderly parents.

One night, as they lay in bed, they heard a thump in their kitchen. "Did you hear that?" Dobson's mother asked.

"Yes, be quiet," his father answered.

As they lay in the darkness, barely breathing, they heard a second thump. Jumping to their feet, they felt their way to the bedroom door, which was closed. Mrs. Dobson, wanting to keep the intruder out, planted her foot against the bottom of the door and braced her shoulder against the upper part.

Mr. Dobson, wanting to confront the unwelcome guest, fumbled for the doorknob and tried to pull the door open. Feeling resistance, he assumed someone was holding the door shut from the outside. Mrs. Dobson, on the other hand, unable to see her husband, assumed the attacker was trying to force the door open. As Dobson tells it, "My parents stood there in the pitch blackness of midnight, struggling against one another and imagining themselves to be in a tug of war with a murderer.''

His mother gave up at that point, released the door and ran to the window to scream for help. As she gathered her strength to yell at the top of her lungs, she noticed a light was on behind her. Turning, she saw that her husband had gone out into the house to look for the intruder—he had been able to go right through once she moved aside.

There had been no prowler at all as things turned out, and certainly no visit from Charles Manson. The Dobsons' emotions had convinced them they were about to be attacked, and they acted accordingly. Logic and experience could have told them there were a dozen possible explanations for the noise they heard, all of them harmless, but their emotions had swept away the quiet voice of reason.[1]

We live in a culture and time that encourage us to live by our feelings rather than reason. ''If it feels good, do it,'' people started saying openly in the 1960s, and the attitude still prevails. ''It can't be wrong, 'cause it feels so right,'' said a popular song of a few years ago. In their marriage vows, many young couples these days do away with the phrase ''till death do us part.'' And in its place they say, ''As long as love [that is, the *feelings* of love] shall last.'' Advertising is geared to grab our emotions and lead us to make impulse buying decisions, and we're bombarded with it from morning to evening.

I don't mean to suggest that our emotions are bad

in and of themselves. They can't be bad, because they're part of the nature God gave us. In fact, they're part of what it means to be made in the image of God. Throughout the Bible we see Him experiencing the same emotions we feel. The parable of the prodigal son in Luke 15, for example, shows God the Father going through sorrow, anxiety, disappointment and great joy.

Anyone who doesn't feel the range of emotions that life's changing circumstances call forth is an incomplete human being. "To everything there is a season," we read in Ecclesiastes, "...a time to weep, and a time to laugh; a time to mourn, and a time to dance" (3:1,4). We'll never know the fullness of joy until we've lived through the depths of despair.

Emotions and the Spiritual Life

Unfortunately, however, acting on the basis of our feelings all too often fuels such sinful compulsive desires as lust, overspending and overeating. And while we don't want to be cut off from our emotions, slavery to them is not God's will for us either. As we read in Galatians 5:22-23, the fruit of the Spirit includes goodness and self-control, not sin and self-indulgence.

Because our emotions are such a big part of us and so important to our behavior, it's not surprising that Satan has worked hard to sell a lie in this area. Sadly, many Christians have believed it. The lie is that in order for our obedience to God's will to be "genuine" and thus acceptable to Him, it has to be "sincere." That is, we have to *feel* like obeying. Our emotions have to be in line with our right behaviors. Otherwise, we're hypocrites. We may do the things we should, but our hearts aren't in it, we think, so our efforts don't count with God.

Now does God want our hearts to be in our service to Him? Yes. Does He want us to have warm feelings toward Him? Of course. As His children, ought we to be motivated more by love for our forgiving Father than by fear? Certainly.

But what exactly is love? More to the point, what does love for God mean? Is it the syrupy sentimentality of movie romances? The best place to find answers is, naturally, the Bible. Its clearest explanation of love, 1 Corinthians 13, contains not a single reference to feelings. And as for the love of God specifically, consider this statement: "For this is the love of God, that we keep His commandments" (1 John 5:3). Jesus said, "If anyone loves Me, he will keep My word; and My Father will love him, and We will come to him and make Our home with him" (John 14:23).

As those verses—and many others I could cite—indicate, the truth is that loving God and pleasing Him have a lot to do with a willingness to obey His commands *regardless of how we feel at the moment*. It has little or nothing to do with warm, gushy feelings. And if we live by our emotions, we risk failing to do that which demonstrates the love He really seeks from us.

To clarify what I mean, let me quote a great Bible teacher of the past who might seem to contradict what I just wrote. His name was Charles Spurgeon, and in his devotional book *Morning and Evening*, writing about Psalm 100:2 (''Serve the Lord with gladness.''), he said, ''Those who serve the Lord with a sad countenance, because they do what is unpleasant to them, are not serving Him at all; they bring the form of homage, but the life is absent. Our God requires no slaves to grace His throne; He is the Lord of the empire of love, and would have His servants dressed in the livery of joy.''

Does God want us to serve Him with gladness rather than grudgingly? Of course. The Bible makes that clear. Out of gratitude for His love, grace and goodness to us, we should be joyful and eager to please Him in all we think, say and do.

But let's be honest: there are times in the week when we're tired, frustrated, or for some other reason especially vulnerable to temptation in the area of compulsive desire with which we struggle. And at those times we may very well not *want* to obey God. Our emotions may be screaming at us to indulge in the sin offered. At midnight, George, whom I described at the beginning of the chapter, can think of a thousand reasons why he *ought* to raid the refrigerator.

So let me ask: at such times of powerful temptation, which would God prefer—that we follow our feelings and indulge in the sin until our desires change, or that we call out to Him for help, admit our feelings aren't what they should be, and with His strength make the decision to turn away from sin? Looking at the choices that way, I think the answer is obvious. The simple truth is that our feelings are not a reliable guide to what we ought to do.

Those who put together the Alcoholics Anonymous program are experts in the treatment of alcoholism because, in part, they're recovering alcoholics themselves. And they have a saying in AA that's very applicable here: "Fake it till you make it." In other words they know that people just starting to get off the bottle will often crave a drink. They'll want a shot of booze more than anything in the world and will be willing to throw away everything, including self-respect and reputation, to get it.

What they *have* to do then (with help) is to *act* as if they *don't* want the drink. They have to remove themselves from the temptation and occupy themselves in some kind of healthy activity—just like people who aren't alcoholics. Eventually, the alcoholics' feelings will change to match their responsible actions—they'll "make it." But until then they have to "fake it" and act as if they don't want to drink.

That's just the way it has to be with all of us, whatever our compulsive desires may be. If we can learn to say no to temptation regularly, our feelings will come around sooner or later, and we'll have the gladness the psalmist wrote about. But we must always be willing to do what God's Word commands regardless of how we feel at the moment. It's too often the case, as a wise person once said, that "temptation is the appeal of the emotions to control the will in opposition to the truth."

Emotions and Beliefs

Besides being vulnerable to sin if we rely on our emotions, we're also likely to wander away from some of our basic Christian beliefs—with potentially disastrous consequences. For example, the Bible assures us that if we confess our sins God will forgive us and cleanse us from all unrighteousness (see 1 John 1:9). The Bible also promises that "as far as the east is from the west, so far has He removed our transgressions from us" (Ps. 103:12).

In spite of such assurances, however, we don't often *feel* forgiven even after we confess our sins, do we? There's lingering guilt, perhaps because we hurt someone in the process of sinning. And then Satan, the great liar, comes in and says, "You're not *really* forgiven, are you? After all, if you were, you'd *feel* better. No, what you did was especially bad, and you haven't earned God's forgiveness yet." When that happens, our tendency is to believe the lie.

But that's just what it is—a lie. *God's Word* is the truth. As we read in Numbers 23:19, "God is not a man, that He should lie, nor a son of man, that He should repent. Has He said, and will He not do it? Or has He spoken, and will He not make it good?" So when our feelings contradict the promise of God that our sins are forgiven, they're lying to us. If we forget that and trust them, we lose the assurance of

God's forgiveness. Then, rather than draw near to Him for help, which is what we should do, we're likely to run from Him in fear.

Speaking of drawing near, another basic Christian belief is that, once we become His children through faith in Jesus Christ, He is always close at hand. In Hebrews 13:5 we read, "For He Himself has said, 'I will never leave you nor forsake you.' " Solomon wrote of the Lord, "There is a friend who sticks closer than a brother" (Prov. 18:24).

Our tendency, however, is to trust our feelings regarding God's nearness to us. In times of spiritual fervor we say, "God feels so close right now. I just know He's with me." And in times of spiritual coldness we say, "God feels so far away. I've lost that sense of closeness I used to enjoy so much."

Yet even those who have had the closest, most consistent walks with the Father have gone through times of difficulty when their feelings could have misled them. The apostle Paul once wrote, "For we do not want you to be ignorant, brethren, of our trouble which came to us in Asia: that we were burdened beyond measure, above strength, so that we despaired even of life" (2 Cor. 1:8). But he could also say in the same letter, "For as the sufferings of Christ abound in us, so our consolation also abounds through Christ" (2 Cor. 1:5).

Jesus Himself, in the night before His arrest, despaired of the suffering He knew lay ahead and asked the Father to let the cup pass from Him. He knew all His disciples would desert Him. And His human emotions were screaming for Him to find a way out of that lonely, painful walk to the cross.

Yet in the end He knew what the Father wanted and we needed, and He said, "Nevertheless not My will, but Yours, be done" (Luke 22:42). I believe He knew He would not go to the cross alone but with the Father, and He could say with confidence as He drew His last breath, "Father, into Your hands I commend My spirit" (Luke 23:46).

Likewise, if we trust God's truth and not our changing emotions, we can know with certainty that from now through eternity the Lord will always be near at hand.

The Problem of Procrastination

Another, very practical problem grows out of living by our feelings. Given the laziness that's a natural part of our sinful human nature, we rarely feel like doing what we should. The result is that many times we fail to do things just because we don't feel like doing them.

Most of us manage to do the things we absolutely have to in order to survive. On any given weekday morning, for example, millions of Americans who would rather stay in bed or go to the beach make their way to the office or the factory instead. They know that doing what they feel like doing would cost them their jobs, which in turn would mean no food, no car, no home, no respect in the community and so on. And when other drivers make them angry on their way to work, they know they can't get away with following their feelings and shooting the offending hot-rodders.

I would guess that most of those millions who force themselves to report to work on time also know they should go to church on Sunday. Yet the majority of them don't do it. Why? What accounts for the difference? The root cause is that for whatever reasons they don't feel like going, and they know they don't have to, so they don't. Besides, there's always next week and the week after that for getting right with God.

Likewise, as Christians we know we should read our Bibles every day, pray, witness and so on. We know we should forgive those who offend us, give liberally and joyfully to the Lord's work, train up our children in the way they should go—and flee from temptation. Yet often we fail to do those things. Why? Because we live by our feelings and so are spiritual procrastinators. We'll start a regular devotional time next week. We'll help our kids memorize Scripture tomorrow. We'll witness to that neighbor next month. We'll look for His way out of our compulsive desires when they stop being so much fun.

Rest assured, Satan loves this approach to Christian living. We can have all the good intentions in the world, and he doesn't care. As long as we live by our emotions and keep putting things off, he's happy. Only when we begin to obey God's commands and do what we should does he tremble.

In times of temptation we need to *expect* our

emotions to work against us. Rather than be surprised by this—rather than trust our feelings to be a true guide toward what we should do—we should cling to the truth of God's Word as our guide. Our feelings will change depending on our circumstances. We can't always control them, turning them on and off at will. But we can stop and ask ourselves if what they're telling us to do is in keeping with what we know God's will to be.

If we find our emotions are in harmony with God's pleasure, well and good. But if they're not, we must choose to do what we know God wants in spite of how we feel. Otherwise, we'll always be slaves to our compulsive desires. Beginning with the next chapter, however, we'll see how God would lead us to freedom.

PART II:
THE VICTORY

SEVEN

FACING THE TRUTH

L isten to a woman who struggled to be free of alcoholism: "[One] of the little monsters I sought to overcome was the monster of *lying*. This was an especially difficult part of my recovery program—to change my deceitful nature into an honest one. The problem is that lying becomes a way of life for the addict. We start by lying to ourselves: I couldn't have done that. I just *wouldn't* behave that way....

"All of life thus becomes a lie. Even my sober times were colored with various shadings of the truth. I was wound about like a mummy with layers and layers of deception. My ears were deaf to the truth; my eyes saw only a miniscule slice of reality.

"When I started working my recovery program, I knew I had to get honest with both myself and other people. Especially with myself....

"At the beginning of my rehabilitation, I promised myself I wouldn't lie for one whole day. It was interesting to see how quickly little fibs and exaggerations tended to creep into my conversation....

"My...daily effort at truthfulness showed me how inclined I was to deny unpleasantness, always to paint the rosy picture. The most staggering realization was how I minimized or lied about my feelings. As my time of sobriety lengthened, real feelings that I had medicated for years started emerging. Unwrapping those endless layers of cover-up was agony. Lies had been my armor, my protection."[1]

Just like that woman, all of us find it difficult to face the painful truth about our weaknesses and failings. And this is never more true than when we're struggling with compulsive desires. We lie to others to protect our reputations, and we lie to ourselves because it hurts so much to look reality in the face.

As A.W. Tozer said, "Of all forms of deception, self-deception is the most deadly, and of all deceived persons the self-deceived are the least likely to discover the fraud." Dostoevsky, the great Russian novelist, said, "Lying to ourselves is more deeply ingrained than lying to others." One writer expressed the same idea with a little humor: "There are times when our self-deception rivals that of the legendary unmarried mother who excused her sin on the ground that her baby was a very small one."

Psychologists who have studied people addicted to gambling have noticed the same key problem: "Compulsive gamblers...have a seemingly limitless capacity for self-delusion, believing that the next bet will result in a big win; that the next bailout will send them on the road to fat city. 'Every time I bought a lottery ticket I was dreaming about what I was going to do with the million dollars,' one recovering gambler says."[2]

The refusal to face the truth and accept responsibility for our actions is nothing new, of course—it's almost as old as the human race. Back in Genesis 3, when Adam and Eve first sinned, God came to them in the garden and confronted them. "Have you eaten from the tree of which I commanded you that you should not eat?" He said (v. 11).

Did Adam then fall to his knees, confess his sin and beg the Lord's forgiveness? No, he did nothing of the sort. He wasn't about to admit the truth of his guilt before a holy God. Instead he said, "The woman whom You gave to be with me, she gave me of the tree, and I ate" (v. 12). In other words, it was all Eve's fault for offering him the fruit. But even more than that, it was *God's* fault because He had brought Eve into his life!

God was patient in trying to get this man and woman to face the truth, so He next asked Eve about her role in the matter. And did she come clean? No, she tried to pass the buck just as her husband did. "The serpent deceived me," she said, "and I ate" (v. 13). That was true as far as it went, but she was trying to deny any personal responsibility for her own sin, and that was a lie.

The Futility of Lying

As difficult as it is to face the awful truth about our compulsive desires, we simply must do it if we're ever to overcome them. We can't expect to gain the victory while we're still denying there's even a serious problem. Admitting we struggle with a compulsive desire is absolutely *the* essential beginning point in any effort to be free. That's why I've made this the first chapter in the "solution" part of the book.

The leaders of the Alcoholics Anonymous program recognize the need for addicted people to face and admit their struggle. That's why when John Doe stands up to speak in an AA meeting, he always begins, "I'm John Doe, and I'm an alcoholic." Those in the program are never allowed to forget the reality of their lives. They're not put down for having a compulsive desire for booze, but they're not allowed to deny the addiction and their responsibility, either.

At the root of all sinful compulsive desires is untruth. Satan comes along and tempts us to believe some lie. He tries to convince us to seek the fulfillment of a legitimate need or desire in an illegitimate way.

In the case of Adam and Eve, God had told Adam that on the day he sinned by eating the forbidden fruit, he would die (spiritually; see Gen. 2:17). In other words, He told Adam to stay away from that tree for his own good. But the devil came to Eve and told her, "You will not surely die" (Gen. 3:4). He then told her God had put that tree off limits only because He wanted to deny her and Adam something good—wisdom. And Eve, followed by Adam, wanted that wisdom and chose to believe in Satan's lie rather than in God's love (see vv. 5-6).

The human mind does some interesting things at a time like that. When we want something so much—in this case godlike wisdom—we lose our objectivity. We play games in our thinking, inventing "good" reasons for going after the thing we want even though, deep down, we still know it's wrong. It's called rationalizing. And if we keep at it long enough, we can justify almost anything to ourselves. That's just what Adam and Eve did. As Tozer put it, "A thing looks morally better because we want it."

The pastor whose story I told back in chapter 3, the one addicted to pornography, also bought into a lie. The women in the pictures seemed to offer warmth and acceptance without the risk of rejection, he said. "But the photos lied," he continued. "I was developing a relationship with ink dots on paper, not with real human beings....Real life is never so easy. Sex comes, for most of us, after months or years of courtship. There is romance, yes, but there is also conflict, and boredom, and incompatibility....Unlike Miss October, [my wife] doesn't spend all day preparing herself to look appealing and available.

"So I am left with an easy lie or a hard truth. The easy lie is the illusion of pornography." Then he concludes, "I was searching for something that could never be satisfied by two-dimensional photos printed on slick magazine paper. And not until I recognized that"—in other words, not until he faced the truth about his situation—"could I begin to turn toward a more appropriate sexual identity."[3]

Once we've accepted the lie that it's OK to sin in order to meet our needs and desires, we're also likely to start believing a lie about God. I mentioned this before, but it bears repeating. Namely, we think of Him not as our loving, forgiving Father but as a kill-joy who likes to see us suffer and is just waiting to jump on us when we sin.

The addicted pastor explains pretty well what happens: "Guilt and fear are such powerful forces that they may also deceive. In my case, they deceived me into seeing God as my enemy....I now view my pilgrimage differently. I believe God was with me at each stage of my struggle with lust....God was present with me even as I fled from Him. At the moment when I was most aware of my own in-adequacy and failure, at that moment I was probably closest to God."[4]

Hitting Bottom

By now I hope the need to face the truth about our compulsive desires is clear. Unfortunately, however, the natural human tendency is to go on denying the truth until we have no choice but to face it. An alcoholic will go on drinking and lying to himself until he smashes his car or, worse yet, kills someone else in an accident. Jimmy Swaggart went right on visiting a prostitute until someone else revealed his secret and the story filled newspaper headlines all across the country.

A Christian psychologist describes the tendency this way: "Change will not begin until the person sees the benefits of self-control and desires to grow up and control his or her own thinking and behavior. This usually does not happen until they 'hit bottom,' when being out of control has become so painful that the process of change looks less painful than not changing."[5]

It seems to take pain of some kind—physical pain, the pain of rejection or humiliation—to cut through the layers of self-deception we've built around our compulsive desires. Only when that pain drowns out the lies are we ready to face the truth.

But let's look at hitting bottom another way. If that's what it takes to wake us up spiritually and put us on the road to victory over sin, it's actually a blessing in disguise. Despite the pain, it's better to hit bottom and straighten out our lives than to continue in sin, apart from God, and maybe also face even worse consequences farther down the path toward self-destruction. That's exactly why a loving God allows us to go through those bottoming-out experiences.

As we read in Hebrews 12, " 'My son, do not despise the chastening of the Lord, nor be discouraged when you are rebuked by Him; for whom the Lord loves He chastens, and scourges every son whom He receives.' If you endure chastening, God deals with you as with sons; for what son is there whom a father does not chasten?...

"Furthermore, we have had human fathers who corrected us, and we paid them respect. Shall we not much more readily be in subjection to the Father of spirits and live? For they indeed for a few days chastened us as seemed best to them, but He for our profit, that we may be partakers of His holiness.

"Now no chastening seems to be joyful for the present, but grievous; nevertheless, afterward it yields the peaceable fruit of righteousness to those who have been trained by it" (vv. 5-7,9-11).

When we have trouble seeing the truth about our compulsive desires, family members can help by forcing us to face it. Drug and alcohol treatment experts have a name for the process—intervention. The idea is that, with a counselor in charge of the meeting, family members state specific behaviors and habits of the person that are clear evidence of his addiction. Then they make it plain that they won't allow things to go on as they have been any longer. They won't pretend there's nothing wrong or cover up for the person.

When this kind of intervention is done, people are often able to begin putting their lives in order without having to hit bottom. However, there's one big potential snag in the intervention process. Before family members can help a loved one with his compulsive desire, *they* have to be willing to face the truth. When

102

a husband or daughter has an addiction, the natural tendency is to try to ignore it, compensate for it within the family, cover it up in front of the world outside, and hope it will go away.

We don't want to believe the worst about a loved one, so we deny the reality of the problem. Although we know better logically, we live as though ignoring it means it doesn't exist. That's why drug treatment counselors find facts such as this: "There's a large discrepancy between the number of kids who use drugs and the number of parents who think their kids use them. The belief that it could never happen to them prevents parents from seeing or acknowledging their children's involvement....But parents who deny the reality keep their kids from getting needed help."[6]

All this means that before we can fully overcome our compulsive desires, *everyone* involved—including family members—has to face the truth squarely. Then, as Jesus said, "You shall know the truth, and the truth shall make you free" (John 8:32).

In Matthew 19:16-22, Jesus tried to help the rich young ruler by doing His own intervention. This young man had at least some desire to be right with God, because he came to Jesus and asked what he needed to do to gain eternal life (and he was wise enough to recognize that Jesus could tell him). When Jesus told him to keep the Ten Commandments, he replied, apparently in truth, that he had been doing so since he was a boy.

This was an exceptional young man. On the surface

at least, he was a very godly person, a model for others to follow. He was probably a better individual than most of the people you know.

But Jesus understood the young ruler had a compulsive desire for money and possessions. He loved them dearly. And Jesus knew he needed to face the truth of that compulsion head on. He needed to realize that at that point he loved material things more than he loved God. So Jesus said to him, "If you want to be perfect, go, sell what you have and give to the poor, and you will have treasure in heaven; and come, follow Me" (v. 21).

Faced with that calling, the young man had to examine his true desires. Which did he want more, to follow the Son of God or to keep his riches? He had to admit he wanted the money more, and he walked away from Jesus.

We can wish the young ruler had decided differently. And who knows? Seeing the truth about himself and wanting eternal life, maybe later on he committed his life to the Savior. I hope we will meet him in heaven some day. But at the time he met Jesus, he chose to stay in his addiction.

Just as Jesus called that young man to face the truth about his sinful compulsion and make a choice for freedom two thousand years ago, so today He calls us to do the same. He wants us to admit our weakness, to reach out to Him and to follow Him on the road to victory. He wants us to choose freedom, to choose life. We'll learn more about making that choice in the next chapter.

EIGHT

COMMITTING THE WILL

Mighty Joshua, the warrior leader, had succeeded Moses and brought the people of Israel
into the promised land. Under his direction they had
fought many battles against heathen enemies, and they
had seen God give them the victory time after time.
Their conquest of the land was almost complete.

But Joshua was now an old man near the end of
his life. Because of his faith in the Lord, he was one
of only two people who had been in the original group
of Israelites that left Egypt and was still alive to cross
the Jordan forty years later. And knowing he was
about to die, Joshua wanted to speak to the people
one last time. So he brought all of Israel together and
gave what we would call a farewell address.

Surely the people's tongues were ablaze with speculation. "Why do you suppose Joshua wants to speak to the whole nation?"

"I don't know, but it must be important."

"Whenever he or Moses called a meeting like this in the past, it was always to give a message from God or to remind us of something God had said or done before."

"Joshua is getting very old, you know. Maybe he's going to tell us what's going to happen after he dies."

"Well, whatever it is, we'll find out soon enough."

So the people gathered to hear the man of God. And what thoughts did he want to leave with them? He reminded them of the marvelous things God had done for them, and he also called their attention once again to the covenant He had made with them. Then he issued a challenge that rings down through the ages—a challenge we need to take up if we want to be free of our compulsive desires.

"Choose for yourselves this day whom you will serve," he said, "whether the gods which your father served that were on the other side of the River, or the gods of the Amorites, in whose land you dwell. *But as for me and my house, we will serve the Lord*" (Josh. 24:15, emphasis added).

Like those Israelites of old, we have to choose each day whom we're going to serve. We have to decide morning by morning—and in the face of every temptation—whether we'll give in to our sinful appetites or obey the Lord. He gave us free will, and we have to exercise it in the right way. The stronger our addictions, the less control we may have over our actions. But even though we may need help sticking with our right decisions, we never lose that basic ability to choose. And we have to use it to commit our lives to God.

Martin Luther used a colorful metaphor to picture this idea. "You can't keep the birds from flying over your head," he said, "but you can keep them from building a nest in your hair." In other words, temptation will always be around us. We can't make it disappear, nor can we deny we often find it appealing. But that doesn't mean we have to give in to it and let it build a comfortable "nest" in our lives.

Another helpful word picture comes from a man named J. Wilbur Chapman, who said: "Temptation is the tempter looking through the keyhole into the room where you are living; sin is your drawing back the bolt and making it possible for him to enter." We can always expect the tempter to be there at the door, peeking in and seductively asking for admittance. He'll tell twenty different kinds of lies if that will convince us to slide back the bolt. But it's our hand on the bolt, and we have to exercise the will—we have to choose whether to let him in or keep him out.

God gave us a tremendous thing in the human will, and it's really much stronger than most of us think. We can do amazing things if we set our minds to it. Consider, for example, the story of William Danforth, the founder of the Ralston Purina Company and a hugely successful businessman. This is how he told his own story:

"As a small boy, before the time of drainage ditches, I lived in the country surrounded by swamp lands. Those were days of chills and fever and malaria. When I came to the city to school, I was sallow-cheeked and hollow-chested. One of my teachers, George Warren Krall, was what we then called a health crank. We laughed at his ideas. They went in one ear and came out the other. But George Warren Krall never let up. One day he seemed to single me out personally. With flashing eye and in tones that I will never forget, he looked straight at me and said, 'I dare you to be the healthiest boy in the class.'

"That brought me up with a jar. Around me were boys all stronger and more robust than I. To be the healthiest boy in the class when I was thin and sallow and imagined at least that I was full of swamp poisons! The man was crazy. But I was brought up to take dares. His voice went on. He pointed directly at me, 'I dare you to fill up your body with fresh air, pure water, wholesome food and daily exercise until your cheeks are rosy, your chest full and your limbs sturdy.'

"As he talked, something seemed to happen inside me. My blood was up. It answered the dare and surged all through my body into tingling fingertips as though itching for battle.

"I chased the poisons out of my system. I built a body that has equalled the strongest boys in that class, and has outlived and outlasted most of them. Since that day, I haven't lost any time on account of sickness. You can imagine how often I have blessed that teacher who dared a sallow-cheeked boy to be the healthiest in the class."[1]

If a boy can commit his will to totally transforming his physical health and then make it happen, surely our wills can help us say no to sinful desires. But we usually give up too easily and too soon. As one pundit said, "The number of times the average man says no to temptation is once weakly." It doesn't have to be that way.

In chapter 4 I talked about how we get caught up in thinking our past failures doom us to fail every time in the future as well. But that's a lie of the devil. As Jesus showed us in the story of the prodigal son, no matter how far down we've fallen, no matter how many times we've given in to our compulsive desires, we can choose to admit our sins and come back in repentance to our forgiving Father.

"I beseech you therefore, brethren, by the mercies of God, that you present your bodies a living sacrifice, holy, acceptable to God," said the apostle Paul (Rom. 12:1). Now I ask you: would Paul command us to do something he knew was beyond our ability? Would he tell us to present our bodies to God if he knew our compulsive desires could overpower our wills and make obedience impossible? Of course not! So after we've faced the truth about ourselves, we need to make this basic commitment of the will to obey the Lord and say no to our addictions.

The Downfall of the Double-Minded

When we make this commitment of the will to godly obedience, it needs to be complete and without reservation. To be double-minded about it—to want to be free and hang on to the sin at the same time—is a prescription for failure and frustration.

The Bible is full of warnings against double-mindedness. Back in 1 Kings 18:21, the prophet Elijah had to challenge the Israelites, "How long will you falter between two opinions? If the Lord is God, follow Him; but if Baal [a false god], then follow him." Tragically, we read next, "But the people answered him not a word."

The psalmist said in Psalm 119:113, "I hate the double-minded, but I love Your law." In other words, wanting our sin and a close relationship with the Lord as well is a detestable attitude.

The apostle James warned, "Cleanse your hands, you sinners; and purify your hearts, you double-minded" (James 4:8).

Jesus Himself told us, "No one can serve two masters; for either he will hate the one and love the other, or else he will be loyal to the one and despise the other" (Matt. 6:24). He also repeated the Old Testament commandment to "love the Lord your God with *all* your heart, with *all* your soul, with *all* your mind, and with *all* your strength" (Mark 12:30, emphasis added).

Clearly, it's futile and even dangerous to be double-minded about our commitment to the Lord. It simply won't work to try to walk with one foot in God's kingdom and the other in the world of sinful indulgence. Thinking we can have it both ways is a lie straight from the pit of hell.

Pastor Erwin Lutzer adds this perspective: "To confess your sins means that you agree with God that you have sinned; it also means that you agree that the sin must be forsaken. Those who confess their sins, intending to repeat the same action, are only partially repentant. Such incomplete repentance leads to a downward spiral of repeated failure. Confession means that you admit your sin and give God permission to remove it from your life. Of course, I'm not saying that you will never commit the same sin again—if so, none of us could claim forgiveness. But there needs to be willingness to part with the sin, and a submission to God's verdict on the matter. Apart from such an acknowledgment, your intentions are self-centered. You are inquiring how forgiveness will benefit you instead of considering how you have offended God."[2]

An insightful person once observed, "What makes resisting temptation difficult for many people is they don't want to discourage it completely." But if we want to be free of our compulsive desires, we must reach a point of willingness to give them up entirely. Until we do, whether by "hitting bottom" or in some other way, we'll only be frustrated, defeated and displeasing to God.

Bought With a Price

As we think about committing ourselves whole-heartedly to the Lord, we should bear in mind that this is not some great sacrifice He's asking us to make. In fact, *He's* the one who made the great sacrifice of His Son on the cross so that we could be free of our compulsive desires. Therefore, when He asks us to give ourselves and our desires to Him, He's only asking for what He deserves.

"Do you not know," Paul wrote to the Corinthian church, "that your body is the temple of the Holy Spirit who is in you, whom you have from God, and you are not your own? For you were bought at a price; therefore glorify God in your body and in your spirit, which are God's" (1 Cor. 6:19-20).

God paid a terrible price to redeem us from our sin. That is why, after telling us to offer ourselves to God as living sacrifices in Romans 12:1, Paul gave this reason: "which is your reasonable service." That is, in light of what God has done for us, giving ourselves one hundred percent to Him is only the right, fair and logical thing to do. To hold on to sinful desires, to serve Him with only halfhearted devotion is wrong, unfair and stupid. As I said earlier, it's also the prescription for spiritual failure.

Let me offer some encouragement at this point, however. Just as giving in to temptation can become a habit, making it easier and easier to sin, so also can *resisting* temptation, making it easier and easier to say yes to God.

As I explained in chapter 3, one of the primary reasons we get hooked into compulsive desires is that we're seeking the fulfillment of legitimate needs, but we're tempted to do it in illegitimate ways. Philosopher Eric Hoffer was right when he said, "Often, the thing we pursue most passionately is but a substitute for the one thing we really want and cannot have." And the one thing every human being wants most of all, whether we realize it or not, is a close, loving relationship with the God who made us for fellowship with Himself.

The good news of the gospel is that we can have that relationship with the Lord. But while we're far from Him, mired in sin, we're liable to grab onto any substitute that comes along. When we make our peace with Him through Christ, however, and draw near, we start to see the substitutes clearly for the cheap imitations that they are. We know the Father and His unconditional acceptance, and we want to please Him more and more. Sin's appeal grows steadily dimmer.

Think of it this way: if a man is starving and you put a piece of raw, rotten meat in front of him, he's likely to gobble it down without much thought. He's consumed with the need for food and isn't in a frame of mind to examine the meat too closely. But a man who's well fed is going to be repulsed by the raw meat. He can see it for what it is, recognize it's dangerous to his health, and make the wise decision to throw it in the trash rather than eat it.

In the same way, when we have a warm relationship

with our heavenly Father, we're able to recognize the falseness and danger of substitutes. And rather than grab for them in desperation, we cling tighter and tighter to the Real.

Help Standing By

Important as it is for us to make the basic commitment of the will I've been talking about in this chapter, we must remember we can only keep that commitment with God's help. I quoted Jesus earlier, from John 15, as saying that we can bear spiritual fruit only as we abide in Him. He is the vine, and we're the branches that draw their life from the vine.

Our Savior is standing by, waiting and eager to help us keep our commitment. Speaking to Christians He said, "Behold, I stand at the door and knock. If anyone hears My voice and opens the door, I will come in to him and dine with him, and he with Me" (Rev. 3:20). If we want the Lord's help, we have only to ask. But He won't force Himself on us. If we do ask, however, we can know for certain He won't let us down.

Back at the beginning of Joshua's tenure as leader of Israel, God gave him this command and promise: "This Book of the Law shall not depart from your mouth, but you shall meditate in it day and night, that you may observe to do according to all that is written in it. For then you will make your way prosperous, and then you will have good success. Have I not commanded you? Be strong and of good courage; do not be afraid, nor be dismayed, for the Lord your God is with you wherever you go'' (Josh. 1:8-9).

Just as God promised to be with Joshua at all times, so He's also with us at all times. The apostle Paul made it clear where he got the strength to live the Christian life: "I can do all things through Christ who strengthens me" (Phil. 4:13). In Colossians 1:29 he wrote, "To this end I also labor [preaching the gospel], striving according to His working which works in me mightily." And in Romans 7, after talking about how he saw the law of sin still at work in himself, he cried out, "O wretched man that I am! Who will deliver me from this body of death?" And then came the answer, "I thank God—through Jesus Christ our Lord!" (vv. 24-25).

The responsibility to commit our wills to obeying God is ours. But if we'll make that commitment, He will strengthen us and guide us in keeping it. And having made it, we'll be ready to start renewing our minds daily, which is the next step in overcoming our compulsive desires.

NINE

DEVELOPING HEALTHY HABITS

In chapter 1, I told of a Christian woman who wrote in Billy Graham's *Decision* magazine about how she almost got caught up in an extramarital affair. Happily, she broke off the relationship before it went that far. And this is how she describes one of the keys to overcoming her compulsive desire for the "other man":

"I realized that my thought-life desperately needed changing. An affair happens in the mind long before it actually occurs....Though it took self-discipline when a lustful thought entered my mind, I refused to let it linger." She analyzed how she used her free time and faced the fact that she had been spending a lot of time reading "trashy novels" (her words) and watching TV soap operas with their bed-hopping characters.

Recognizing the bad influence on her mind, she changed her habits. "During the time I ordinarily spent watching television, I now started Bible study, something I had been neglecting. The verses I read provided spiritual strength, something to fall back on when tempted."[1]

That woman's experience illustrates clearly the next step we need to take on the path to freedom from our sinful compulsive desires. As she said, our actions grow out of our thoughts. There's an old saying that carries the unmistakable ring of truth: "Sow a thought, reap an action. Sow an action, reap a habit. Sow a habit, reap a life." And we control the thoughts we sow—the thoughts we continually allow our minds to dwell on—by what we choose to put into our brains.

Knowing that, we can reprogram our minds by putting in only good things instead of negative influences like "trashy novels." And in turn we'll also develop healthy habits to replace the old, unhealthy ones that feed our compulsive desires.

Right after calling for us to offer our bodies to God as living sacrifices in Romans 12:1, Paul wrote, "And do not be conformed to this world, but *be transformed by the renewing of your mind*, that you may prove what is that good and acceptable and perfect will of God" (Rom. 12:2, emphasis added). Only as we renew our minds in the way I've just described are we changed into people who can know and do God's will.

In the same book Paul gave this explanation of the importance of what we let our minds dwell on: "For those who live according to the [sinful] flesh set their minds on the things of the flesh, but those who live according to the Spirit, the things of the Spirit. For to be carnally minded is death, but to be spiritually minded is life and peace. Because the carnal mind is enmity against God; for it is not subject to the law of God, nor indeed can be. So then, those who are in the flesh cannot please God" (Rom. 8:5-8).

This theme is so crucial to Christian living that Paul went back to it again and again. In Colossians 3:1-2 he put it this way: "If then you were raised with Christ, seek those things which are above, where Christ is, sitting at the right hand of God. *Set your mind on things above, not on things on the earth*" (emphasis added).

Paul was so determined to guard the gate to his mind that he described himself as "bringing every thought into captivity to the obedience of Christ" (2 Cor. 10:5). As far as he was concerned, there's no such thing as a stray thought. Every thought helps to shape the people we are, either for good or for evil.

The Replacement Principle

How do we make all this happen practically: taking our thoughts captive, renewing the mind and developing healthy habits rather than sinful compulsions? I alluded to the key earlier; I call it the replacement principle.

Simply put, it's not enough to try to get rid of our sinful thoughts and sinful desires. We can't just force them out of our minds and expect them to stay gone. Our brains are always active and focused on something, so as soon as we push a thought out, another will come in immediately to take its place. And if we're not careful, that new thought will be another sinful one.

To illustrate what I mean, picture a blue ball in your mind's eye. Now think about it for a minute—its size, how hard or soft it is, whether its surface is rough or smooth, its weight and so on. After you've thought on those things for a minute or two, try to force all thoughts of the ball out of your mind. Banish the image and all those characteristics of the ball from your thoughts. Go ahead and try that.

What happened when you tried to force all thoughts of the ball from your brain? Were you able to do it? It probably wasn't easy if you were. But even if you could do it, what took place in your mind when you did? Did your brain go blank—empty of all thought? Did a test pattern appear in your mind's eye like the one a TV station shows when it goes off the air late at night?

I'm joking, of course, but my point is that your mind certainly did *not* go blank when you forced out thoughts of the blue ball. If you were able to do that at all, thoughts of some other kind came into your mind the instant the image of the ball went out. Our brains are always working, and our minds are never blank. They're always focused on something. This is why it's not enough to force sinful thoughts from our minds; we have to replace them with good, God-honoring thoughts.

Jesus talked about the futility of just trying to push the evil out of our lives. "When an unclean spirit [or desire] goes out of a man," He said, "he goes through dry places, seeking rest; and finding none, he says, 'I will return to my house from which I came.' And when he comes, he finds it swept and put in order. Then he goes and takes with him seven other spirits more wicked than himself, and they enter and dwell there; and the last state of that man is worse than the first" (Luke 11:24-26).

Like the evil spirit of which Jesus spoke, the sinful thoughts that fuel our compulsive desires will keep coming back. And if they haven't been replaced by better thoughts that leave no room for the negative, they'll take up residence again and lead us right back into the mess we were in before. We might even end up worse off than we were previously, burdened by feelings of further guilt, frustration, failure and hopelessness.

Think back to the woman writing in *Decision* magazine: she couldn't just drive lustful thoughts from her mind. She had to quit reading the books and watching the shows that fed those thoughts. And in their place, in the time she used to spend on them, she started studying her Bible again after having neglected it for some time.

Notice that earlier she had replaced a good influence (the Bible) with bad ones (trashy novels and

TV soap operas). The results had been marital infidelity in the form of lusting after the other man (see Matt. 5:27-28), and almost a full-blown affair that might have destroyed her marriage forever. Only when she reversed that process and replaced the bad influences with the good did she come to her senses, avoid the affair and restore her marriage.

No doubt Paul had this replacement principle in mind when he wrote, "Finally, brethren, whatever things are true, whatever things are noble, whatever things are just, whatever things are pure, whatever things are lovely, whatever things are of good report, if there is any virtue and if there is anything praise-worthy—meditate on these things" (Phil. 4:8). These are the kinds of things that must fill our minds if we really want to be free of our compulsive desires.

Out With the Old, In With the New

Putting the replacement principle to work in our lives involves several action steps. First, we have to stop doing the things that have gotten us into trouble. If compulsive shopping is the problem, for example, this might mean we stop window shopping as a form of recreation. It might mean we stop browsing in certain magazines that feature ads for products we can't resist. As a Dutch proverb says, "What the eye sees not, the heart craves not." It doesn't take much thought to recognize the things we need to stop doing, whatever our individual compulsions may be.

Second, we must be prepared to quit doing the

negative things *immediately*. We don't dare try to kid ourselves into thinking we can give them up gradually, a little bit at a time. It just won't work that way. The longer we let negative thoughts and habits hang on, the longer it will be before we're finally free. "You cannot play with the animal in you without becoming wholly animal," said Dag Hammarskjold, the late leader of the United Nations who was also a Christian. "He who wants to keep his garden tidy doesn't reserve a plot for weeds."[2]

The best way to get rid of a sinful thought pattern or habit is to choose a specific quitting time and then just drop it once and for all at that point. We don't procrastinate. We don't give the devil the chance to talk us out of it or to sell us the lie that we can overcome it gradually just as well. It won't be easy. It will be painful. Any change in our lives is difficult, even when we know it's for the better. But we must make up our minds that we're going to quit doing what we know is bad for us and stick with it. The rewards will come in God's good time.

The writer to the Hebrews offered us Jesus' example as encouragement in this struggle: "For consider Him who endured such hostility from sinners against Himself, lest you become weary and discouraged in your souls. You have not yet resisted to bloodshed, striving against sin" (Heb. 12:3-4).

Third, we need to replace the negative with a positive. And the best positive I can think of—the influence that best matches Philippians 4:8—is God's Word, the Bible. A passage I quoted earlier in the

123

book is worth repeating here: "How can a young man [or anyone else] cleanse his way? By taking heed according to Your word....Your word I have hidden in my heart, that I might not sin against You" (Ps. 119:9,11).

God's Word is a fantastic weapon in our spiritual warfare. "For the word of God is living and powerful, and sharper than any two-edged sword, piercing even to the division of soul and spirit, and of joints and marrow, and is a discerner of the thoughts and intents of the heart" (Heb. 4:12).

Hiding God's Word in our hearts so its power can work on our behalf means we must first of all memorize it. That way it's instantly available to us whenever we need it, whether we're driving the car, in the office, taking care of the kids or anywhere else. We don't have to have a Bible at hand and the time and freedom to go searching through it for what we need.

Whatever the compulsive desires we need to overcome, we begin by making a list of verses related to them. If overeating is the problem, for example, we might include verses like these: "But I discipline my body and bring it into subjection, lest, when I have preached to others, I myself should become disqualified" (1 Cor. 9:27).

"For the drunkard and the glutton will come to poverty, and drowsiness will clothe a man with rags" (Prov. 23:21).

"The young lions lack and suffer hunger; but those who seek the Lord shall not lack any good thing" (Ps. 34:10).

124

If the problem is lust, some of the good verses to memorize would be these: "You have heard that it was said to those of old, 'You shall not commit adultery.' But I say to you that whoever looks at a woman to lust for her has already committed adultery with her in his heart" (Matt. 5:27-28).

"Can a man take fire to his bosom, and his clothes not be burned? Can one walk on hot coals, and his feet not be seared? So is he who goes in to his neighbor's wife; whoever touches her shall not be innocent" (Prov. 6:27-29).

"Flee also youthful lusts; but pursue righteousness, faith, love, peace with those who call on the Lord out of a pure heart" (2 Tim. 2:22).

As you can see, the Bible is full of passages that speak directly to our sinful compulsive desires. A concordance and topical Bible are good places to find them.

Once we've memorized verses that speak to our needs, we can put them to use. When temptation comes, we recite the verses to ourselves, and the reminder of God's truth will give us strength to stand firm. As often as the temptations come, we repeat our verses. Believe me, if there's one thing Satan doesn't want to do, it's inspire us to learn and repeat Scripture!

I'm not saying this process of memorizing and reciting the Bible will make our sinful desires go away. The sin nature and the devil don't give up that quickly. But the more we feed the spiritual meat of God's Word into our minds, the stronger we'll grow.

Sin's appeal will fade, and our love for God and the desire to please Him will increase. Our habits will also reflect the life of the Savior more and more.

Computer programmers have an acronym that summarizes this process beautifully: GIGO. It stands for "Garbage in, garbage out." In other words, what you get out of a computer in the way of accurate information is only as good as the information you put into it. If you put garbage in, you can't expect the computer to transform it miraculously into something else. You'll get nothing but garbage back out. On the other hand, if you put good, accurate information in, you'll get the same in return.

Just so with us. If we feed garbage like immoral TV shows into our minds, we'll get sinful thought patterns and slavery to compulsive desires as a result. But if we feed God's Word into our minds, we'll get healthy thoughts and Christlike habits in return.

Pastor Chuck Swindoll tells a story that illustrates how memorized Scripture can help us say no to temptation. He was in Canada one time on a speaking trip and had been away from home for eight days, with two more to go. He was lonely and had been feeling sorry for himself during a hotel dinner he ate alone. Starting back to his room, he bought a newspaper and looked through the sports section. It was full of hockey news and nothing else, and he doesn't care much for hockey.

As he walked toward the elevator, he noticed a couple of young women laughing and talking on the phone in the lobby. He smiled as he passed, waited a bit for the elevator, then got on. So did the two young women. He pushed the button for the sixth floor, where his room was. Then, noticing the women didn't reach for the control panel and wanting to be polite, he asked them, "What floor?"

One of them looked at him invitingly and said, "How about six? Do you have any plans?"

The three of them were alone on the elevator, in Canada, and he was lonely and flattered by their attention. He was tempted, and he had a vital decision to make. This is what he says next: "Do you know what immediately flashed into my mind? My wife and children? No, not at first. My position and reputation? No, not then. The possibility of being seen or set up? No.

"God gave me an instant visual replay of several Scripture verses:

> Do not be deceived, God is not mocked; for whatever a man sows, this he will also reap (Gal. 6:7);

> Put on the full armor of God, that you may be able to stand firm against the schemes of the devil (Eph. 6:11, NASB); and

> Even so consider yourselves to be dead to sin, but alive to God in Christ Jesus. Therefore do not let sin reign in your mortal body that you should obey its lusts (Rom. 6:11,12, NASB).

"During that elevator ride, the memorized Word flew to my rescue. Right on time.

"As I looked back at the two, I replied, 'I've got a full evening planned already; I'm not really interested.' They looked at me like I was Mork from Ork as I stepped off the elevator (and they stayed on!). I walked to my room, suddenly grateful for the overcoming power of God's Book.''

Swindoll goes on to conclude, "As I write these words to you, I am filled with renewed strength because His Word has kept me faithful again and again for twenty-five years of marriage. Yes, the memorized Word works.''[3]

As we fill our minds with biblical truth through daily reading, study and memorization, we'll be more and more able to offer testimonies like Swindoll's. God's Word is just as powerful in our lives as in his. The same Holy Spirit who brings that Word into his thoughts at times of need (see John 16:13) will do the same for us. And our thoughts and desires will grow ever more like those of the Lord. We'll look closer at Jesus, our supreme example, in the next chapter.

TEN

FOLLOWING CHRIST'S MODEL

One of the great soul-winning evangelists of the last century was D.L. Moody, a man who had started adult life as a shoe salesman in Boston. Thousands of people were saved under his ministry, revivals grew out of his crusades in Great Britain and America, and the Bible school he started in Chicago still produces many missionaries year after year—a lasting legacy. What inspired this great man of God? What sparked his extraordinary efforts in the Lord's service?

The story is told of how young Moody was in England on one occasion when he heard a speaker remark, ''The world has yet to see what God will do with a man fully consecrated to Him.'' That challenge struck Moody like a shot and forced him to his knees. There he resolved that with the Lord's help he would be that man.

Although Moody was already working full-time in Christian ministry, it was right *after* he made that decision and became consumed with preaching the gospel that his crusades began to bear such incredible fruit. Within just a few years he was known widely on both sides of the Atlantic.

So far in this book I've spoken of compulsive desire only in a negative light, equating it with sin. But it needs to be said here, as we've just looked at the replacement principle for renewing our minds, that there's also such a thing as a godly obsession. We can rightly get excited about and give our lives over to some things. Moody's determination to be completely committed to the Lord and His work is a good example of this.

Wrongful Obsessions

But just as Moody made a conscious decision to be totally devoted to God, it's also possible to make a deliberate choice for a wrongful obsession. Much of the pain in human history has been caused by people who did exactly that.

The French emperor Napoleon, for instance, was obsessed with the desire to conquer the world for his own vain glory. He plunged Europe into war for years at a time on several occasions in an effort to fulfill his ambition. Alexander the Great had the same obsession and succeeded in conquering all the known world of his time. Then he wept because there were no more nations to subjugate.

Nero, a Roman emperor in the early years of the Christian church, was obsessed with the satanic desire to wipe out Christianity. When half of Rome was burned in a great fire in A.D. 64, Nero blamed it on Christians (probably to cover his own guilt) and began the first great persecution of the church. Thousands of believers were tortured and murdered as a result.

Adolf Hitler was obsessed not only with the age-old dream of world domination, but also with a hatred for and a determination to wipe out God's chosen race, the Jews. He destroyed those Christians, too, who dared to oppose his evil plans.

In our own day, in everyday life, we have people who haven't just been deceived into seeking the fulfillment of their legitimate needs in illegitimate ways. Instead they've chosen to be obsessed with desires for power over others or an overabundance of material possessions.

Jesus' Magnificent Obsession

There's a better way, however: that of our Lord Jesus. He, too, had an obsession—a magnificent obsession. Unlike the men mentioned above, He sought nothing for Himself. Pride, greed and lust for power had no place in Him. Instead, as the angel announced to the shepherds on the night of His birth,

"Do not be afraid, for behold, I bring you good tidings of great joy which will be to all people. For there is born to you this day in the city of David *a Savior*, who is Christ the Lord" (Luke 2:10-11, emphasis added).

Jesus Himself said, "For I have come down from heaven, not to do My own will, but the will of Him who sent Me....And this is the will of Him who sent Me, that everyone who sees the Son and believes in Him may have everlasting life; and I will raise him up at the last day" (John 6:38,40).

He came to save us from our sins, and He was prepared to pay the terrible price required to do that—"the Lamb slain from the foundation of the world" (Rev. 13:8). Though He knew the cross awaited Him, "He steadfastly set His face to go to Jerusalem" (Luke 9:51), and nothing would stop Him. He also said, "Therefore My Father loves Me, because I lay down My life that I may take it again. *No one takes it from Me, but I lay it down of Myself*" (John 10:17-18, emphasis added).

Finally, when Jesus was being arrested in the Garden of Gethsemane and His disciples tried to defend Him with weapons, He told them, "Do you think that I cannot now pray to My Father, and He will provide Me with more than twelve legions of angels? [But] how then could the Scriptures be fulfilled, that it must happen thus?" (Matt. 26:53-54).

He was obsessed with accomplishing the Father's will and doing the work of saving a sinful world. No one forced Him to go to Calvary, and no one could.

He lay down His life of His own free will.

Jesus' compulsion was magnificent because no one else could do what He did. To take our place on the cross, our substitute had to be sinless, and only Jesus was. If He had been unwilling for whatever reason, we would have been without hope. Only He could save us, and praise God He was willing!

Jesus' obsession was also magnificent because it was so selfless. He ministered long and hard and had no home to call His own. He suffered hatred and misunderstanding and cruel, unjustified abuse. Yet even from the cross He prayed for His tormentors, "Father, forgive them, for they do not know what they do" (Luke 23:34). Rather than receiving the worship and love He deserved, He gave all He had for us, up to and including His very life. This was without doubt the most amazing and wonderful act in human history.

Jesus' Call to Us

It's no wonder that Jesus' loving sacrifice has inspired more books, songs and speeches than any other event. There's nothing to compare with it. But His marvelous obsession wasn't meant only to win our salvation and gratitude. It was also meant to inspire us as an example.

Jesus is seeking those who will be obsessed with His desire—to do the Father's will and take the gospel to people everywhere—even if it means enduring the same kind of pain and misunderstanding heaped on

133

Him at the crucifixion. "You will be hated by all for My name's sake," Jesus said (Matt. 10:22), but that won't happen if we hide our faith and continue in slavery to our sinful desires. In that case we'll look no different from the rest of the world, we'll accomplish nothing for the Lord, and the world will have no reason to hate us. But the One whose opinion really matters, who loves us so much that He gave His only Son, will be grieved deeply by our betrayal.

The hearts of people throughout the world today are tossing about on the stormy sea of doubt, sickness, worry, confusion and misunderstanding. Until our hearts are filled with the same obsession Christ had, however, we won't be able to bring His peace and comfort to this troubled planet. Our hearts must be so yielded to Him that His power flows through us. And when our hearts are truly in tune with His, we'll become part of the ongoing fulfillment of *His* magnificent obsession.

The apostle Paul was so full of God's love and a desire to see people saved that preaching the gospel became a compulsion to him. "For if I preach the gospel, I have nothing to boast of," he said, "for necessity is laid upon me; yes, woe is me if I do not preach the gospel!" (1 Cor. 9:16). And when he preached, whether it was before the common people or governors and kings, the truth came pouring out of him like a Niagara Falls. He was overwhelming!

One time he was having to defend himself to Festus, the Roman governor of Palestine, and the Jewish king Agrippa. And after Paul had given his personal testimony of coming to faith in Christ, Festus cried out, "Paul, you are beside yourself! Much learning is driving you mad!" (Acts 26:24). He wasn't going crazy, of course. Festus couldn't tell the difference between madness and the anointing of the Holy Spirit. But Paul was so obsessed with presenting the gospel that that's how he sometimes came across to unbelievers.

Paul had given up a position of high leadership in Judaism to preach Christ, but he considered the loss as rubbish (see Phil. 3:4-10). And the people of the churches he founded and visited loved him. Even today we name our sons Paul because of his example. What an honor and a legacy!

In the last few years of my own ministry we've had a God-given compulsion to feed the poor. We believe He doesn't want His children in the Third World to starve. So we've put hundreds of hours of effort into launching an operation to help feed those starving masses. We won't reach everyone, but many lives are being saved that wouldn't be otherwise.

Truly, God can inspire and guide our positive compulsive desires. He can fill them with the Holy Spirit and use them to bless others.

Being used by God is certainly a worthy replacement for sinful compulsions! But beware! Our adversary, Satan, will oppose us every step of the way. So now let's look more closely at how to resist his influence in our lives.

ELEVEN

RESISTING SATANIC INFLUENCE

The time was the exciting early days of the New Testament church. Jesus had been crucified, buried and resurrected. Multitudes had seen and heard Him alive, and many had even touched Him. Then He had ascended into heaven, followed by the coming of the Holy Spirit with power into the lives of Jesus' disciples. And beginning with Peter's bold sermon on the day of Pentecost, the church in Jerusalem was growing rapidly.

Besides meeting spiritual needs with the gospel, the church was also ministering to the physical needs of believers. We read in Acts 4:34-35, ''Nor was there anyone among them who lacked; for all who were possessors of lands or houses sold them, and brought the proceeds of the things that were sold, and laid them at the apostles' feet; and they distributed to each as anyone had need.''

Into this scene came a man named Ananias and his wife, Sapphira. They appear to have had a genuine desire to follow Christ, because Acts 5 leads us to conclude they were a part of the church. That means they had made a profession of faith in Jesus as the Messiah, which was still not a popular thing to do in Jerusalem. In addition they, like many others, sold a piece of land they owned with the intention of giving the money to the church. That was a good thing to do, and no one made them do it. It was their free-will decision.

Their devotion to the Lord and His church was halfhearted, however, and Satan knew it. So he planted this idea in Ananias's head: ''You received X amount of money for the land—think what you could do with all that money, or even part of it! Does the church really need all of it? After all, many others are giving, too, which means there's plenty to go around. So what's the harm in keeping part of the money for your own use? Besides, you've worked hard all your life, and you'll get only this one chance to sell that land. Shouldn't you reward yourself just a little?''

This idea appealed to Ananias, and he decided he *would* keep part of the proceeds for himself. Then Satan planted this idea in his mind: ''You know, it might be embarrassing to take the money to the apostles and say you got X amount for your land and are only giving Y amount to the church. That could make you look selfish, even though *you* know you deserve to keep a little for yourself. So why don't you say Y is the total amount you got for the land? Who will know any different or be hurt by the lie? It's just a small, innocent deception, and it will help to keep everyone happy.''

Unfortunately, Ananias bought into the lie, and his wife also agreed to go along with the deception. But God was not fooled. When Ananias brought the money to the apostles and told his lie about how much he had received from the sale of the land, Peter said, ''Ananias, why has Satan filled your heart to lie to the Holy Spirit and keep back part of the price of the land for yourself? While it remained, was it not your own? And after it was sold, was it not in your own control? Why have you conceived this thing in your heart? You have not lied to men but to God'' (Acts 5:3-4).

It's a well-known story, and you probably recall that Ananias proceeded to fall down dead. A bit later, when Sapphira repeated the lie to Peter, she also died on the spot (vv. 5,7-10). Not surprisingly, ''great fear came upon all the church and upon all who heard these things'' (v. 11).

My point in retelling this story is to note how Satan worked in the situation. As I said, Ananias and Sapphira apparently were Christians. But they also had a love of money, ''a root of all kinds of evil'' (1 Tim. 6:10) and a problem God no doubt would have worked to replace with a greater love for

Himself if they had lived. But Satan was also aware of their spiritual weakness in this area, and he's an expert at exploiting such weaknesses. So he planted the idea of lying in Ananias's heart, careful to do it in such a way that Ananias thought it was his own idea. (After all, even a carnal Christian is likely to oppose an idea if he knows it's coming from the devil.)

Not only did Satan make Ananias think the lie was his own idea, but he also deceived him into believing it was OK to lie. Just as he got Adam and Eve to think it was a good idea to disobey God and eat from the forbidden tree because it would make them wise, so he got Ananias to think everyone would come out ahead if he lied about the proceeds from his land sale.

This is a standard tactic of the devil. "When he speaks a lie, he speaks from his own resources, for he is a liar and the father of it," Jesus said (John 8:44). For this reason we have to keep our thinking clear by anchoring ourselves in the Word of God, as I discussed in the last chapter. It's the only way we can recognize when Satan is trying to convince us that sin—including our compulsive desires—isn't bad and may even be spiritual.

One of the jobs of U.S. Treasury agents is to catch and stop counterfeiters. To do that, agents have to recognize a counterfeit bill when they see one. And the Treasury Department has found that the best way to train its agents for this task is to make them thoroughly familiar with *genuine* bills. That way, they know so well what the real thing looks like that they're able to spot fake bills immediately. They can see instantly when the printing isn't quite right or the wrong kind of paper was used.

In the same way, when we know God's Bible thoroughly, we're able to spot Satan's lies instantly. Immersing ourselves in Scripture is a much more effective—not to mention spiritually profitable—way to be lie detectors than studying Satan's lies themselves. But we must always be on guard, never forgetting that Satan is a brilliant liar. This is why Paul wrote to the Corinthian Christians, "But I fear, lest somehow, as the serpent deceived Eve by his craftiness, so your minds may be corrupted from the simplicity that is in Christ" (2 Cor. 11:3).

Our great enemy is constantly working to destroy marriages (see 1 Cor. 7:5). He blinds the spiritual eyes of the unsaved (see 2 Cor. 4:4) and causes people to forget the truth of the gospel even when they hear it (see Luke 8:12). And as long as he can keep our hearts divided and our minds confused, he can also keep us wrapped up in our compulsive desires, spiritually ineffective and dishonoring to the Lord.

Know Your Enemy

As we think about how to resist Satan's influence, it's important to understand first just what he is. He's not a god, and he's not the Lord's equal. Like us he's a created being. But he's not human; he's an angel. He was one of the cherubs assigned to cover, or guard, the very throne of God (see Ezek. 28:14), and he was especially attractive to look at.

But Satan wasn't content to serve in the presence of God. "You [Satan] were perfect in your ways from the day you were created, till iniquity was found in you," Ezekiel tells us. "Your heart was lifted up because of your beauty; you corrupted your wisdom for the sake of your splendor" (28:15,17).

Isaiah described Satan's incredible pride this way: "How you are fallen from heaven, O Lucifer, son of the morning! How you are cut down to the ground, you who weakened the nations! For you have said in your heart: 'I will ascend into heaven, I will exalt my throne above the stars of God; I will also sit on the mount of the congregation on the farthest sides of the north; I will ascend above the heights of the clouds, I will be like the Most High' " (14:12-14).

Revelation 12:4 suggests that, when Satan rebelled against God, he took a third of the angels with him. I ask you: If he could convince a third of God's own angels to try to overthrow Him, what can he do to relatively weak (compared to angels) human beings?

But while Satan is actively opposing God's work for the time being, his fate is sealed, and he's a doomed rebel. "Yet you shall be brought down to Sheol, to the lowest depths of the Pit. Those who see you will gaze at you, and consider you, saying: 'Is this the man who made the earth tremble, who shook kingdoms, who made the world as a wilderness and destroyed its cities, who did not open the house of his prisoners?' " (Is. 14:15-17).

The apostle John, looking into the future under the

Holy Spirit's inspiration, wrote, "And the devil, who deceived them [people who help him in the end times], was cast into the lake of fire and brimstone where the beast and the false prophet are. And they will be tormented day and night forever and ever" (Rev. 20:10).

It's not just in the future that Satan will be defeated, either. Jesus' resurrection dealt him a crushing blow (see Col. 2:15). And because we're in Christ, we share in that victory (see Rom. 6). This is why James could write, "Therefore submit to God. Resist the devil and he will flee from you. Draw near to God and He will draw near to you" (4:7-8). God would not give us an instruction we couldn't obey. So if we submit to God and draw near to Him, Satan *will* flee. Here again is the principle of embracing a good as an essential part of getting rid of an evil.

Paul said in Ephesians 4:27, "Do not give the devil a foothold" (NIV). And in Romans 12:21 he commanded, "Do not be overcome by evil, but overcome evil with good." What these verses suggest, along with James 4 and many others, is that we *can* say no to Satan. He is *not* our master. We can stand fast against the temptations and lies he brings our way, "because He who is in you is greater than he who is in the world" (1 John 4:4).

Satan knows all this, too, but that doesn't mean he's going to give up easily. In fact, he tries to trick us into thinking we're still—and always will be—slaves to our compulsive desires. Unfortunately, he has managed to deceive many Christians into thinking victory in Christ is only a fantasy instead of the daily reality it *can* be.

Author Larry Christenson shows this reality clearly by picturing Satan as "The Old Landlord": "Think of yourself as living in an apartment house. You live there under a landlord who has made your life miserable. He charges you exorbitant rent. When you can't pay, he loans you money at a fearful rate of interest, to get you even further into his debt. He barges into your apartment at all hours of the day and night, wrecks and dirties the place up, then charges you extra for not maintaining the premises. Your life is miserable.

"Then comes Someone who says, 'I've taken over this apartment house. I've purchased it. You can live here as long as you like, free. The rent is paid up. I am going to be living here with you, in the manager's apartment.'

"What a joy! You are saved! You are delivered out of the clutches of the old landlord!

"But what happens? You hardly have time to re-joice in your new-found freedom when a knock comes at the door. And there he is—the old landlord! Mean, glowering and demanding as ever. He has come for the rent, he says.

"What do you do? Do you pay him? Of course you don't! Do you go out and pop him on the nose? No—he's bigger than you are!

"You confidently tell him, 'You'll have to take that up with the new Landlord.' He may bellow, threaten, wheedle and cajole. You just quietly tell him, 'Take it up with the new Landlord.' If he comes back a dozen times, with all sorts of threats and arguments, waving legal-looking documents in your face, you simply tell him once again, 'Take it up with the new Landlord.' In the end he has to. He knows it, too. He just hopes that he can bluff and threaten and deceive you into doubting that the new Landlord will really take care of things."[1]

As Christenson points out, Satan is a powerful enemy. He's not someone to trifle with. It's foolish to try to defeat him alone—that will only end in disaster, because "he's bigger than you are." That's why we draw near to God through prayer and His Word and tell Satan to talk to Jesus if he thinks he has some claim on our lives. We don't win spiritual battles with carnal, human solutions, but by laying hold of the very power of the Almighty. As a wise person once said, "Calling on Jesus to help you overcome temptation may look weak to men. But the demons and their boss know it is their undoing."

To give us an idea of Satan's power, consider the New Testament book of Jude. It speaks of apostasy and conflict between God's angels and those who follow the evil one. We read in verse 9, "Yet Michael the archangel [one of God's chiefest and most powerful angels], in contending with the devil, when he disputed about the body of Moses, dared not bring against him a reviling accusation [on his own], but said, 'The Lord rebuke you!' "

When Moses, the man of God died, "He [God] buried him in a valley in the land of Moab, opposite

Beth Peor; but no one knows his grave to this day" (Deut. 34:6). Apparently when that happened, Satan tried to steal away Moses' body, perhaps to defile it in some way out of hatred since Moses had been such a thorn in his side. And Michael was there to protect the body. But by himself he couldn't withstand the devil, so he had to invoke the name of the Lord.

If that was true of God's archangel, how much more true will it be of us? Indeed, in my many years of ministry in foreign lands, I've cast demons out of people numerous times, and I can tell you from firsthand experience that I'm not the one who makes the demons leave. Only calling upon the Lord and His sovereign power in prayer makes them go away, just as Jesus told His disciples (see Mark 9:14-29).

Spiritual Armor

As much as we need God's help, however, let's not forget that God also expects us to do our part. Long before we get to the point of saying no to Satan and his temptations, we can be saying yes to God by preparing for the battles that are sure to come. How? By putting on the spiritual armor He has provided.

"Put on the whole armor of God, that you may be able to stand against the wiles of the devil. For we do not wrestle against flesh and blood, but against principalities, against powers, against the rulers of the darkness of this age, against spiritual hosts of wickedness in the heavenly places. Therefore take up the whole armor of God, that you may be able to withstand in the evil day, and having done all, to stand.

"Stand therefore, having girded your waist with truth, having put on the breastplate of righteousness, and having shod your feet with the preparation of the gospel of peace; above all, taking the shield of faith with which you will be able to quench all the fiery darts of the wicked one. And take the helmet of salvation, and the sword of the Spirit, which is the word of God" (Eph. 6:11-17).

The truth he's talking about is the truth of God's Word. Jesus said, "If you abide in My word, you are My disciples indeed. And you shall know the truth, and the truth shall make you free" (John 8:31-32).

The breastplate of righteousness is a life-style of joyful commitment to godly standards. When all our ways are ordered by God, the devil has no sinful or uncontrolled habits he can grab hold of and use to drag us into the bondage of compulsive desires.

The gospel of peace is the good news that no matter how many times we fall, Jesus has made our peace with the Father. Failure is never permanent, and we have a divine power source to draw on if we only will.

The shield of faith is our assurance that no matter what temptation we're going through, no matter how hard the struggle, and no matter what our feelings tell us at the moment, God is with us, He loves us, and obeying His commandments is always the way to true happiness and lasting joy.

Knowing we've been saved—bought with the price of Jesus' blood so that we're no longer our own—keeps our thinking and our priorities clear. It's the helmet of salvation. And the sword of the Spirit, God's Word, cuts right through all of Satan's lies and our own rationalizations, laying bare our motivations and longings.

Prepared with this kind of spiritual armor, we can go forward in the name of our Lord, expecting to win. But if there are any chinks in our armor, be sure Satan will find them out and concentrate all his efforts in those places of vulnerability.

Jesus' Example

One of the better known passages of the Bible is the devil's temptation of Jesus in the wilderness. We find the story in Luke 4:1-13. And in that story we see a beautiful example of how to resist satanic influence.

It's a fascinating account, because Satan knew Jesus was fully God, but also fully man. That means, among other things, that He got tired and hungry and angry and discouraged just like the rest of us—but without sin. Satan was determined to try to change that last fact if he could. And the Holy Spirit led Jesus to the place, apparently to help Jesus, the man, mature in His devotion to the Father through the time of testing.

Jesus fasted during His forty days in the desert, so naturally He grew quite hungry. And being a man, He might also have grown a little discouraged, wondering if the Father was really with Him. Satan appealed to both of these weaknesses when he said, "If You are the Son of God, command this stone to become bread" (v. 3).

The Savior certainly could have given such a command, and the stone would have been transformed instantly. But doing so would have shown a lack of faith in the Father's love and perfect will. Jesus knew the Father had a more important purpose for Him in that time and place than just filling His belly and demonstrating His divine nature to the devil (who already knew exactly who He was).

So Jesus answered with Scripture that conveyed this higher priority: "It is written, 'Man shall not live by bread alone, but by every word of God' " (v. 4).

Next Satan tried to bribe Jesus with an offer of something he knew Jesus wanted: authority over all the earth (see vv. 5-7). All Jesus had to do was get down on His knees and worship the devil.

Jesus knew there were two things terribly wrong with such a suggestion. First, the Father had laid out a far different way for Him to win authority over all the world, and that way led to a cross (see Eph. 1:19-23). To grab at Satan's offer would have been a rejection of God's will and an attempt to escape the cross. Second, of course, the Lord had commanded thousands of years before, "You shall have no other gods before Me...you shall not bow down to them nor serve them. For I, the Lord your God, am a jealous God" (Ex. 20:3,5).

Accordingly, Jesus was outraged at Satan's

suggestion and said, "Get behind Me, Satan! For it is written, 'You shall worship the Lord your God, and Him only you shall serve' " (v. 8).

Finally, Satan tried to deceive Jesus by misusing Scripture. If you've ever doubted the devil knows how to quote the Bible in a twisted but appealing way to serve his own ends, just look at verses 9-11. Again addressing Jesus' human pride and fears, he challenged Him to give a cheap demonstration of His divinity. That would have accomplished nothing except to make Jesus a puppet of the evil one.

Once again Jesus answered with Scripture that reflected the truth of God's Word, not just the letter: "It has been said, 'You shall not tempt the Lord your God' " (v. 12).

In every temptation Jesus responded with scriptural truth—not passages chosen to deceive and manipulate, but passages rightly divided to reflect God's will. In this way He drew near to God through the Word hidden in His heart and mind, and the devil had to give up and leave. And in the same way we, too, can find victory over the devil.

Hanging Tough

There's one more lesson we need to learn from Jesus' example in Luke 4, and that's the necessity of persistence. Even when we do everything we should, victory won't come easily. I've already spoken of how Satan likes to keep coming back to try to regain control of our lives, and that was certainly Jesus' experience. But Jesus "hung tough," and we need to do the same. No matter how many times the devil brings temptation into our lives, no matter how many times he tries to convince us we'll never escape our compulsive desires, we need to stand firm in the Lord and His truth.

Look at Luke 4:2: Jesus was led into the wilderness by the Spirit and "tempted for forty days by the devil." All during those forty days—even before the three temptations described in detail—Satan was enticing Jesus with one appealing offer after another. Then came the three temptations at a time when Jesus had to be near exhaustion.

As if all that weren't enough for Jesus to have to cope with, we read at the end of the story, "Now when the devil had ended every temptation, he departed from Him *until an opportune time*" (v. 13, emphasis added). In other words, though Satan left at that point and gave Jesus some relief, he kept his eye on Him and stayed ready to jump at the next chance to tempt Him. He wasn't going to give the Savior a moment's peace if he could help it.

But, praise God, Jesus stood fast against every temptation! He won the victory with the help of the Father and the spiritual armor He provides, and we can as well. Satan is a powerful, deceitful enemy who would love nothing more than to keep us enslaved to sinful compulsive desires. But the Lord who loves us and yearns for us to enjoy His freedom is stronger still.

TWELVE

SEEKING HELP

Toward the end of World War II, American bombers were dropping tons of explosives on Japan continually in an effort to drive the Japanese to their knees in surrender. The Japanese, of course, tried to shoot down the planes with antiaircraft guns. And on June 1, 1945, one particular American B-29 bomber took a direct hit from a flak shell over Tokyo. Half the plane's nose was shot away.

The pilot, still strapped in his cockpit seat, was dead. The copilot, his left arm hanging useless and blood covering his body, struggled to control the huge plane. All his gauges were knocked out, so he had no idea of his speed, direction or altitude.

He was helpless to find his way back to base on

the island of Iwo Jima, which U.S. Marines had taken from the Japanese just a couple of months before. Yet to bail out of the crippled plane over enemy territory would mean certain capture or death for the entire crew.

Just when all hope seemed lost, two American P-61 Black Widow night fighter planes appeared out of the blue. Taking up positions on each side of the bomber, they guided the battered aircraft all the way back some seven hundred miles to a safe landing on Iwo Jima.

Almost forty years later, in 1984, the crew members from the three planes met for a reunion in California. There they remembered that day when life seemed lost for the bombers until comrades in arms came alongside to do for them what they could not and lead them to safety.[1]

Just as the men on that bomber needed help to return to base in one piece, so we need help in overcoming our compulsive desires.

While it's possible for some (a very few) people to summon up enough willpower to overcome sinful compulsions on their own—at least for a time—most of us need help, and that's the way God intends it to be.

By ourselves it's just too easy to be deceived by Satan, to get lazy, to tire of the struggle or to think we've got it made when there's still some distance to go. But with the right kind of help our chances for lasting success are many times better

The Help of Fellow Christians

One kind of help we need comes from fellow believers who know us and with whom we have regular, in-depth discussions. Small-group Bible studies are an excellent place for this, although friendships and good Sunday school classes can also provide the right setting.

The fact is that God made us all to be part of one body, dependent on one another (see 1 Cor. 12). We need one another, and we're to care for each other. "A new commandment I give to you," Jesus said, "that you love one another; as I have loved you, that you also love one another. By this all will know that you are My disciples, if you have love for one another" (John 13:34-35). "Bear one another's burdens, and so fulfill the law of Christ," taught the apostle Paul in Galatians 6:2. "Iron sharpens iron, so one man sharpens another" (Prov. 27:17, NASB). And the apostle James added, "If you really fulfill the royal law according to the Scripture, 'You shall love your neighbor as yourself,' you do well" (2:8).

How, specifically, do we help one another overcome our compulsive desires? One way is simply by meeting together to talk about what's going on in our lives and to encourage one another. "And let us consider one another in order to stir up love and good works, not forsaking the assembling of ourselves together, as is the manner of some, but exhorting one another, and so much the more as you see the Day approaching" (Heb. 10:24-25).

There's a tendency, when we're struggling with a compulsive desire, to think we're all alone in the world—to imagine we're the only one who can't get victory over our particular weakness. But when we come together and share honestly, we learn we're *not* alone. That knowledge by itself is some comfort.

But we also get much more than that: other believers tell us what's been most helpful to them in gaining victory. We get challenged anew to live for the Lord—our motivational batteries are recharged. Our hope is renewed that with God's help we *can* replace sinful compulsions with godly desires. And other Christians who've gone through the same struggles can show us more clearly where we've been deceived by Satan's lies.

Besides encouragement and the wisdom of those with more experience, we also need and can receive unconditional acceptance from one another. The devil wants us to believe that, if we struggle with—and often fall into—a particular sin, God gives up on us and condemns us. Unfortunately, we Christians often seem bent on proving Satan correct, because we're quick to condemn each other. (Someone once observed that the church is the only outfit that shoots its own wounded.)

But Jesus warned us sternly against such an attitude: "Judge not, that you be not judged. For with what judgment you judge, you will be judged; and with the same measure you use, it will be measured back to you. And why do you look at the speck in your brother's eye, but do not consider the plank in your own eye? Or how can you say to your brother, 'Let me remove the speck out of your eye'; and look, a plank is in your own eye? Hypocrite! First remove the plank from your own eye, and then you will see clearly to remove the speck out of your brother's eye" (Matt. 7:1-5).

Instead of judging one another when we're earnestly seeking to live for the Lord, we should be forgiving and restoring each other. Jesus made it plain that God takes this matter very seriously: "For if you forgive men their trespasses, your heavenly Father will also forgive you. But if you do not forgive men their trespasses, neither will your Father forgive your trespasses" (Matt. 6:14-15).

The apostle Paul, in writing to the Corinthians about their need to forgive someone, gave this extra reason: "Now whom you forgive anything, I also forgive. For if indeed I have forgiven anything, I have forgiven that one for your sakes in the presence of Christ, *lest Satan should take advantage of us; for we are not ignorant of his devices*" (2 Cor. 2:10-11, emphasis added).

One of Satan's favorite tactics for dividing believers and destroying churches is to build within them a spirit of unforgiveness over some offense or other—often something pretty minor when you look at it objectively. I could tell sad story after sad story of fellowships that were torn apart by an unwillingness to forgive and forget, and chances are that you could, too. But this isn't the place for that. Instead, my point here is that when we follow biblical teaching and forgive one another as we should, admitting we're *all* imperfect and have our own struggles with sin, the church becomes a place that offers the wonderful acceptance we need to face our struggles *honestly* and find help to overcome them.

A man named Peter DeVries hit the nail on the head when he said, "We are not primarily put on this earth to see through one another, but to see one another through."

Along with encouragement and acceptance comes accountability, and this can be tremendously helpful. Suppose, for example, that your compulsive desire is for food. You eat too much when you're hungry, and you snack on fattening foods even when you're not. As a result you weigh more than you should, and your efforts to lose weight are halfhearted and short-lived at best. But if you make yourself accountable to another person or a support group, your chances for success increase greatly.

Let's say you agree that, each week when you meet with your group, you'll tell them about each time you went off your diet in the last seven days. You'll also tell them how much weight you lost or gained in that period. Would knowing you have to give such a report in three days help you to resist that late-night bowl of ice cream? You bet it would! This is why weight-loss programs that include accountability are far more successful than plans you try to stick with on your own.

Accountability is also the key to the success of groups like Alcoholics Anonymous. At least once a week, members meet together to admit their weakness, talk about what's going on in their lives and draw strength from one another. Each new member is also paired with an experienced member of the program, one who serves as a mentor and can be called upon day or night for help in resisting the temptation to drink. This individual accountability often means the difference between success and failure both in the immediate moment of craving alcohol and in the long term.

Likewise, an individual or group to which we're accountable can help us say no to temptation, whatever our compulsive desires may be.

A final way fellow Christians can help is by praying for us, and this may be the most important of all. God hears and answers the prayers of united believers. Jesus said, "Again I say to you that if two of you agree on earth concerning anything that they ask, it will be done for them by My Father in heaven" (Matt. 18:19). The apostle James wrote, "Confess your trespasses to one another, and pray for one another, that you may be healed. The effective, fervent prayer of a righteous man avails much" (5:16).

There's a trememdous blessing in hearing someone lift you up before the Lord. It can be much more hope-producing than praying alone. In fact, it can make all the difference in the world.

A Christian woman named Susan was planning to take her own life in the fall of 1972. She was deeply depressed and unhappy with her life, and suicide seemed the only way out. Two of her children were rebellious, and her husband, instead of being supportive, seemed insensitive. She felt alone and helpless. Her only relief was in tranquilizers and sleeping pills. She finally reached the point of giving up.

On the day she planned to kill herself, Susan decided almost by "accident" to go to a women's meeting at her church. Once there, she didn't take part in the singing but wept silently. Nor did she eat any of the lunch that followed. Another woman invited her to the prayer room for counsel, however, and Susan struggled mightily over the question of whether she should go. She hadn't planned on telling anyone what she was about to do.

Finally she went, and four other women joined her. They read the Bible with her and then prayed. On their knees they called on the Lord to deliver Susan from the desire to destroy herself, and they asked Him to give her strength for the trials in her home. For an hour Susan struggled with her emotions while the women prayed.

At the end of that time Susan was a changed person. No longer did death seem the only or even the best way to deal with her problems. "I had never felt so alive in all my life," she said. Her struggles didn't just disappear, of course, but she now knew without a doubt that God was on her side. "Even though Satan has buffeted me a number of times," she wrote, "I can say that God does all things well, because truly His power is shown in weakness. I do have a health problem—but the depression is gone."[2]

Prayer is simply *the* most powerful resource we have, and when we pray for one another, God does wonderful things in response. He delights to do this for His children!

Encouragement, wisdom, accountability and prayer from fellow Christians—these are powerful aids in overcoming our compulsive desires. God truly blessed us when He baptized us into a body of believers who could support one another. This kind of fellowship, not surprisingly, is the key to the phenomenal growth of the world's largest church—Yoido Full Gospel Church in Seoul, Korea, pastored by Paul Yonggi Cho.

Known as home cell groups in Cho's church, these fellowships include every member of the church and consist of fifteen families or fewer. Pastor Cho explains what takes place when they get together: "Each week these members gather in their neighborhood cell meetings, where they have an opportunity to worship the Lord, to pray together, to learn from the Word, to experience the working of the gifts of the Holy Spirit, to see miracles and healings and to enjoy loving relationships with their fellow Christians."[3]

As a result, Cho says, "The members of Full Gospel Church are enthusiastic. They are experiencing revival 365 days a year."[4] And when we find that same kind of fellowship with other Christians, we, too, can enjoy revival every day. We'll *feel*, not just know intellectually, the truth of what Jesus said in Matthew 18:20: "For where two or three are gathered together in My name, I am there in the midst of them."

Help From the Lord

I've been saying it all through this book, but it bears repeating one more time: the Lord is the one indispensable element in any victory over compulsive desires. Apart from Him, all our efforts are worthless and doomed to failure. But "with God all things are possible" (Matt. 19:26).

We've already seen how important God's Word is to our success. In addition God gave us His Holy Spirit as an incredible resource for daily life. Jesus told His disciples near the end of His time on earth, "It is to your advantage that I go away; for if I do not go away, the Helper will not come to you; but if I depart, I will send Him to you...[W]hen He, the Spirit of truth, has come, He will guide you into all truth" (John 16:7,13).

Paul said simply, "Walk in the Spirit, and you shall not fulfill the lust of the flesh. For the flesh lusts against the Spirit, and the Spirit against the flesh; and these are contrary to one another, so that you do not do the things that you wish" (Gal. 5:16-17). Isn't that the essence of compulsive desire—that we find ourselves repeatedly doing something we know we shouldn't yet feel powerless against?

Next Paul lists some of the works of the flesh, and it's a list full of compulsive sins: "adultery, fornication, uncleanness, licentiousness, idolatry, sorcery, hatred, contentions, jealousies, outbursts of wrath, selfish ambitions, dissensions, heresies, envy, murders, drunkenness, revelries, and the like" (Gal. 5:19-21).

Now notice the total contrast: "But the fruit of the Spirit is love, joy, peace, longsuffering, kindness, goodness, faithfulness, gentleness, *self-control*" (Gal. 5:22-23, emphasis added). Those are exactly the things we're looking for in seeking freedom from our compulsive desires, aren't they? And they're the result of the Spirit's working in our lives.

So Paul concludes, "If we live in the Spirit, let us also walk in the Spirit" (5:25). In the same vein, Paul wrote in Ephesians 5:18, "And do not be drunk with wine, in which is dissipation; but be filled with the Spirit." That means that moment by moment we lean on Him and draw on His limitless strength, knowing our own is not enough but that His is *more* than enough.

Another way the Spirit helps us is that when we're struggling with our compulsive desires, we often don't know just how we should pray. Our understanding of God's plans and purposes tends to be hazy at such times, because we're focused on wanting nothing more than immediate relief from the trial. So Paul wrote, "The Spirit also helps in our weaknesses. For we do not know what we should pray for as we ought, but the Spirit Himself makes intercession for us with groanings which cannot be uttered. Now He who searches the hearts knows what the mind of the Spirit is, because He makes intercession for the saints according to the will of God'' (Rom. 8:26-27).

In other words, part of the job the Father gave the Spirit is to pray for us continually. Isn't that fantastic! It thrills my soul to know that the Holy Spirit of God, a member of the divine Trinity, is interceding for me day in and day out, making up for the lack in my own prayers.

Not only does the Spirit pray for us, but so also does our Savior. ''He [Jesus] is also able to save to the uttermost those who come to God through Him, since He ever lives to make intercession for them'' (Heb. 7:25). And remember that, when Jesus prays for us, He does so out of an intimate, personal knowledge of what we're going through: ''For in that He Himself has suffered, being tempted, He is able to aid those who are tempted'' (Heb. 2:18).

Praise God, we are not alone! The Spirit and the Son stand with us. ''What then shall we say to these things? If God is for us, who can be against us?'' (Rom. 8:31). Who indeed?

The Lord also helps us through His Word by reminding us of who He is and who we are—He is the creator God, worthy of our reverence and fearsome in His wrath against sin, and we are His creation. As those facts are made clear time and again in the Scriptures, we are motivated afresh to seek His way and yield our wills to His. ''The fear of the Lord is a fountain of life, to avoid the snares of death,'' wrote Solomon (Prov. 14:27).

This reverent yieldedness to the Father's plan and His priorities was Jesus' attitude in the Garden of

Gethsemane when He prayed, "Father, if it is Your will, remove this cup from Me; nevertheless not My will, but Yours, be done" (Luke 22:42). And in everything God brings into our lives or allows to come in, His overriding purpose is to make us ever more like Jesus. "For whom He foreknew, He also predestined to be conformed to the image of His Son, that He might be the firstborn among many brethren" (Rom. 8:29).

Perhaps, then, we would do well to consider a thought from a saint of days gone by, Thomas Wilcocks, concerning our struggles with compulsive desires: "In all thy temptations, be not discouraged. Those surges may be, not to break thee, but to heave thee off thyself, onto the Rock of Christ."

If our compulsive desires serve that purpose, we may find God has used them for our *good*. Maybe then we'll better understand the truth of Romans 8:28: "And we know that all things work together for good to those who love God, to those who are the called according to His purpose." And maybe then we'll be more eager to obey the command of 1 Thessalonians 5:16-18: "Rejoice always, pray without ceasing, in everything give thanks; for this is the will of God in Christ Jesus for you."

NOTES

Chapter 2: Desires We Can't Control

1. Jean Seligmann, "Helping Fight Against Extra Helpings," *Newsweek*, December 5, 1988, p. 78.
2. Constance Holden, "Against All Odds," *Psychology Today*, December 1985, p. 34.
3. *Ibid.*
4. William Backus and Marie Chapian, *Why Do I Do What I Don't Want to Do?* (Minneapolis: Bethany House, 1984), pp. 43-44.

Chapter 3: Why We Become Enslaved

1. Anonymous, "The War Within Continues," *Leadership*, Winter 1988, pp. 30,33.
2. Stephen Arterburn and Jim Burns, *Drug-Proof Your Kids* (Pomona, Calif.: Focus on the Family, 1989), p. 26.
3. *Ibid.*, p. 27.
4. Ron Blue, *The Debt Squeeze* (Pomona, Calif.: Focus on the Family, 1989), pp. 17-18.
5. *Ibid.*, p. 16.

Chapter 4: How Our Desires Control Us

1. Erwin Lutzer, *How to Say No to a Stubborn Habit* (Wheaton, Ill.: Victor, 1979), p. 34.
2. *Ibid.*, pp. 33-34.
3. *Ibid.*, pp. 36-37.
4. *Ibid.*, pp. 132-133
5. *Ibid.*, pp. 57-58.
6. *Ibid.*, p. 48.

Chapter 5: Why Doesn't God Free Us Instantly?

1. Ron Lee Davis, *Gold in the Making* (Nashville: Nelson, 1983), p. 28.
2. Stephen Brown, *If God Is in Charge* (Nashville: Nelson, 1983), p. 48.

Chapter 6: Emotions: Help or Hindrance?

1. James Dobson, "Human Emotions: Friends or Enemies?" booklet (Pomona, Calif.: Focus on the Family, 1989), pp. 4-5.

Chapter 7: Facing the Truth

1. Sandra Simpson LeSourd, *The Compulsive Woman* (Old Tappan, N.J.: Chosen, 1987), pp. 172,173.
2. Constance Holden, "Against All Odds," *Psychology Today*, December 1985, p. 34.
3. Anonymous, "The War Within Continues," *Leadership*, Winter 1988, pp. 30,31,33.
4. *Ibid*:, p. 27.
5. Richard P. Walters, *Counseling for Problems of Self-Control* (Waco, Tex.: Word, 1987), pp. 17-18.
6. Stephen Arterburn and Jim Burns, *Drug-Proof Your Kids* (Pomona, Calif.: Focus on the Family, 1989), pp. 107-108.

Chapter 8: Committing the Will

1. William Danforth, *I Dare You!*, quoted in Dale Galloway, *Dare to Discipline Yourself* (Minneapolis: Jeremy Books, 1980), pp. 20-21.
2. Erwin Lutzer, *How to Say No to a Stubborn Habit* (Wheaton, Ill.: Victor, 1979), pp. 48-49.

Chapter 9: Developing Healthy Habits

1. Maureen Grant, "I Was Not Immune. Temptation Did Come," *Decision*, January 1988, p. 17.
2. Quoted in Charles R. Swindoll, *Three Steps Forward, Two Steps Back* (Nashville: Nelson, 1980), p. 96.
3. *Ibid.*, pp. 100-101.

Chapter 11: Resisting Satanic Influence

1. Larry Christenson, *The Renewed Mind* (Minneapolis: Bethany Fellowship, 1974), pp. 41-42.

Chapter 12: Seeking Help

1. Jack Gulledge, *Inspirational Talks* (Nashville: Broadman, 1986), pp. 34-35.
2. Erwin Lutzer, *How to Say No to a Stubborn Habit* (Wheaton, Ill.: Victor, 1979), pp. 110-111.
3. Paul Yonggi Cho, *Successful Home Cell Groups* (Plainfield, N.J.: Logos, 1981), pp. 50-51.
4. *Ibid.*, p. 52.